WHO'S WHO IN FAULKNER

WHO'S WHO IN

FAULKNER

MARGARET PATRICIA FORD
SUZANNE KINCAID

LOUISIANA
STATE
UNIVERSITY
PRESS

PREFACE

This volume includes a character index with brief identifications of key people who inhabit the fictional world of William Faulkner. The value of such an index should be apparent to anyone who has read a Faulkner novel, and twice as apparent to one who has read two. Faulkner once commented, "I remember the people, but I can't remember what story they're in nor always what they did. I have to go back and look at it to unravel what the person was doing. I remember the character, though." (*Faulkner in the University*, 49). It is hoped that this index will be useful both to the beginning reader of Faulkner and to the reader who has a long-standing acquaintance with the Snopeses, Sutpens, and Sartorises.

We have attempted to make it even more useful by including cross references and nicknames. Some explanation concerning the format and content of the entries should be noted. Married women are listed by the name of their last husband, as, for example, Stevens, Melisandre Backus Harriss. Sources in which the character may be found are listed at the end of the entry, the novels arranged according to date of publication. The entry itself consists of pertinent known data regarding the character's ancestry, occupation, personality, and actions—enough to enable the reader to bring the character into focus or to refresh his memory, but not enough to insure him of a full understanding of the character, a goal which may be reached only by reading the works themselves. Dates listed in the index and in the genealogies are those for which there is positive evidence in the fictional works. No attempt has been made to hypothesize or to project or to reconcile possible variants. In rare instances the abbreviation for *circa* is used preceding a date when the context has indicated that the event concerned almost certainly occurred within that year; when there exists a possibility of more than a year's variance, no liberties have been taken. Variants in data from the text of *Absalom, Absalom!* and the accompanying "Chronology" and "Genealogy" in the Modern Library Edition are duly noted. Faulkner himself readily admitted the presence of conflicting data in his Yoknapatawpha saga. He sometimes changed names and physical traits of characters, and confused dates and places. Such conflicts may be annoying to the literal-minded reader, but the authors, although fully alive to the intriguing challenge of making consistent the tangled relationships and dates, prefer to play the game by Faulkner's rules of order. Finally, Faulkner's own words are incorporated (set off in quotation marks) in many of the entries.

The biographical sketch is included as a brief summary of the facts of Faulkner's life. The lack of any full-length biographical study and the plethora of folklore surrounding his life tend to increase the difficulties of making more extended biographical statements.

M.P.F. and S.M.K.

CONTENTS

WHO'S WHO IN FAULKNER

BIOGRAPHICAL SKETCH

Among the influences that shaped the writings of William Faulkner were: (1) the family legends passed down to him; (2) Faulkner's apprenticeship and his brief association with literary circles in New York and New Orleans; and (3) the Mississippi world in which the author lived most of his life. The stories of his family and the historically charged air which Faulkner breathed as a boy became the materials for such novels as *The Unvanquished, Sartoris,* and parts of the Snopes trilogy. Faulkner's apprenticeship and his associations with other young writers produced *Soldiers' Pay, Mosquitoes,* the New Orleans sketches, and such stories as "Beyond," "Fox Hunt," and "Divorce in Naples," works that are clearly less significant in the Faulkner canon. The third influence, the land and its people, was without a doubt the greatest one. For from Faulkner's incredible memory of orally propagated tales and his physical and moral proximity to his region grew the major body of his work. Each of these influences is important enough to be considered in detail; together they form the intricate texture which Faulkner turned into fiction.

I

Faulkner's concern with the past was not merely the result of reading history. As a boy he seemingly absorbed the Civil War legends and stories about his own great-grandfather, Colonel William C. Falkner, from the people of north Mississippi.

> They didn't talk so much about that war, I got that from the maiden spinster aunts which had never surrendered. But I can remember the old men, and they would get out the old shabby grey uniforms and get out the old battleflags on Decoration, Memorial Day. Yes, I remember any number of them.[1]

By far the most illustrious of Faulkner's ancestors and, in addition, one of the most illustrious men in that part of the state, was William C. Falkner (the *u* was added later by his great-grandson and namesake). Anyone who has read *The Unvanquished* is already familiar with the career of Colonel Falkner, who is thinly disguised in the novel as Colonel John Sartoris. Colonel Falkner was born in East Tennessee, but lived most of his life in Ripley, Mississippi, where he died in 1889 after being shot down on the streets of the town by a former partner in the railroad which he had built. As a young man the Colonel had served in the Mexican War; later he fought for the Confederacy. A lawyer and landowner, he was also the author of several books, among them a popular novel, *The White Rose of Memphis*.[2]

Colonel Falkner's son by his first marriage was John Wesley Thompson Falkner, sometimes called "the Young Colonel." A lawyer like his father, and later a banker, he was the father of three children, one of them Murry C. Falkner.

William Faulkner, the novelist, was born September 25, 1897, in New Albany, Mississippi, the oldest of the four sons of Murry C. and Maud Butler Falkner. About 1902 the family moved to the nearby college town of Oxford, where Murry Falkner owned a livery stable. Later he went into the hardware business, and afterward held several positions in the business administration of the University of Mississippi.[3]

As a child, William Faulkner was probably influenced by the Falkner Negro nurse-mammy, Caroline Barr (1840–1940), to whom he later dedicated *Go Down, Moses.* Both Dilsey, of *The Sound and the Fury,* and Aunt Callie, of *The Reivers,* are at least partial fictional portraits of this loyal family servant.

Faulkner's schooling was sporadic. He did not graduate from high school, but early determined to be a writer, and read extensively, from about 1914 advised and assisted by his friend Phil Stone, to whom he later dedicated all three volumes of the Snopes trilogy.

In 1918 Faulkner served briefly with the Royal Air Force in Canada, but was still in training at the time of the Armistice. After the war he returned to Oxford and was enrolled as a special student at the University of Mississippi. He excelled in French and Spanish, but received *F* and *D* in two semesters of English.

About this time Faulkner made his first trip to New York City at the invitation of the writer and critic Stark Young, a fellow Mississippian. In New York, he stayed with Young, who found him a job as a clerk in Lord and Taylor's bookshop. The shop was managed by Elizabeth Prall, who later became Sherwood Anderson's wife. Here formed the beginnings of contacts which would be renewed and enlarged later in New Orleans among the Andersons and other literary people.

II

Although Faulkner sometimes referred to himself as a farmer, not as a literary man, he himself has indicated the importance of the influence these literary friends in New York and, more especially, in New Orleans, had on his writings.

Faulkner returned to Oxford and in 1921 took a job as postmaster at the University of Mississippi—a job which he filled until he resigned October 31, 1924. His resignation included the now well-known remark, "As long as I live under the capitalistic system I expect to have my life influenced by the demands of monied people. But I will be damned if I propose to be at the beck and call of every itinerant scoundrel who has two cents to invest in a postage stamp." Late in 1924 he brought out his first book of poems, *The Marble Faun*, with an introduction by Phil Stone. The poems received little critical notice, and the volume little financial success. With the money he had saved as postmaster, Faulkner left Oxford for New Orleans, en route to Europe. But instead of leaving immediately, he remained in New Orleans for six months. It was at this time that a series of sketches and short stories appeared in the New Orleans *Times-Picayune* and a "little magazine," *The Double-Dealer*. It was also during this period that Faulkner wrote his first novel, *Soldiers' Pay*, which was brought out the following year (1926) by Sherwood Anderson's publisher.

Besides Anderson and his wife, others in the New Orleans literary circle included Roark Bradford, then an editor of the *Picayune*; Lillian Friend Marcus, managing editor of *The Double-Dealer*; John McClure, reviewer for both publications; Hamilton Basso, who was then studying at Tulane; Lyle Saxon and H. L. Mencken. Basso has commented on the New Orleans group:

> If I never much hankered after Paris during the expatriate years, it was because, in the New Orleans of that era, I had Paris in my own back yard. It was my privilege to be on companionable terms, not only with Faulkner, but with all those who made the French Quarter a sort of Creole version of the Left Bank. We weren't a literary clique, we weren't a movement, and God knows we weren't a school. What held us together was simply mutual friendship and good will.[4]

In an interview, Faulkner once described the source of his income while he was in New Orleans:

> And I was in New Orleans, I worked for a bootlegger. . . . I ran a launch from New Orleans across Pontchartrain down the Industrial Canal out into the Gulf where the schooner from Cuba would bring the raw alcohol and bury it on a sand-spit and we'd dig it up and bring it back to the bootlegger and his mother—she was an Italian, she was a nice little old lady, and she was the expert, she would turn it into Scotch with a little creosote, and bourbon. We had labels, the bottles, everything—it was quite a business.[5]

Another of Faulkner's acquaintances in New Orleans was William Spratling, the artist, with whom he sailed for Europe on

July 7, 1925, aboard the freighter *West Ivis*. About that trip Faulkner later recalled, "I knew Joyce, I knew of Joyce, and I would go to some effort to go to the cafe that he inhabited to look at him. But that was the only literary man that I remember seeing in Europe in those days." [6]

Faulkner returned to the United States, to Lafayette County, Mississippi, before the end of 1925. The exact results of his brush with literary circles cannot be calculated. It would seem, though, that he had become a not unrecognized writer and was learning the tools of his craft. He had only to return to his county to recognize the materials which he would use for his major fiction.

III

Yoknapatawpha County, with its county seat at Jefferson, was the setting of Faulkner's next novel, *Sartoris*. Faulkner told Jean Stein in an interview:

> Beginning with *Sartoris* I discovered that my own little postage stamp of native soil was worth writing about and that I would never live long enough to exhaust it, and that by sublimating the actual into the apocryphal I would have complete liberty to use whatever talent I might have to its absolute top. It opened up a gold mine of other people, so I created a cosmos of my own. [7]

Faulkner wrote steadily for the rest of his life. Once he commented, "I intend to live to be at least a hundred and I'll probably still be writing." [8] During 1929 and 1930, two of his major works appeared: *The Sound and the Fury* and *As I Lay Dying*. Also during the late twenties he began the stories that became *The Hamlet*, not published until 1940. But at this time, his writings were still showing little profit. He worked in Oxford as a sign painter, then found a job in the electric power plant. On June 20, 1929 he married Estelle Oldham Franklin, who had two children by her first marriage. Estelle Oldham was a childhood sweetheart of Faulkner's, had married a lawyer named Cornell Franklin and divorced him in 1928. Faulkner has said that the added responsibilities of a family intensified his writing activity at that point. It is interesting to note his description of the writing of *As I Lay Dying*:

I got a job in the power plant, on the night shift, from 6 P.M. to 6 A.M., as a coal passer. I shoveled coal from the bunker into a wheelbarrow and wheeled it in and dumped it where the fireman could put it into the boiler. About 11 o'clock the people would be going to bed, and so it did not take so much steam. Then we could rest, the fireman and I. He would sit in a chair and doze. I had invented a table out of a wheelbarrow in the coal bunker, just beyond a wall from where a dynamo ran. It made a deep, constant humming noise. There was no more work to do until about 4 A.M., when we would have to clean the fires and get up steam again. On these nights, between 12 and 4, I wrote *As I Lay Dying* in six weeks, without changing a word. I sent it to Smith and wrote him that by it I would stand or fall.[9]

Faulkner has also commented about his writing of *Sanctuary* at this time. His reply to the question, "Why did you write *Sanctuary?*" was, "I needed money, and I wanted to buy a horse and I thought that people made money writing books, so I wrote a book to make enough money to buy that horse." [10] *Sanctuary* did not show a profit, however—at least not immediately. Faulkner wrote what he has called a "potboiler," sent it off to Jonathan Cape and Harrison Smith and, when he received the galleys for proof-reading, decided to rewrite the whole thing. The plates had already been made, but the publisher offered to pay half for new ones. Faulkner said:

I got a job passing coal to earn the $270 to pay my half for the plates to print the book and then the publisher went bankrupt. I didn't get any money at all. So I did the best I could with the book. It was in a way already in the public domain, I couldn't throw it away and I rewrote it and did the best I could with it.[11]

In the thirties he published six novels, *Sanctuary* (1931), *Light in August* (1932), *Pylon* (1935), *Absalom, Absalom!* (1936), *The Unvanquished* (1938), and *The Wild Palms* (1939); a second collection of short stories, *Doctor Martino and Other Stories* (1934); and a volume of verse, *A Green Bough*. In addition, he placed dozens of short stories with magazines.

In 1932, after the filming of *Sanctuary*, called in the movie version, *The Story of Temple Drake*, Faulkner began accepting scenario work in Hollywood. Working with Howard Hawks and Nunnally Johnson, he adapted *Today We Live* from one of his short stories, helped write *The Road to Glory* (1936), and adapted for film *Slave Ship* (1937), *The Big Sleep* (1946), and Ernest Hemingway's *To Have and Have Not*. In 1949 he advised in the production of *Intruder in the Dust*, which was filmed on location in Lafayette County.

In 1950 it was announced that Faulkner was to be the fourth American to receive the Nobel Prize for literature. The honor, following fairly close on the heels of Malcolm Cowley's influential *Portable Faulkner* (1946), marked the beginning of wide critical acceptance of his novels.

Before the Nobel Prize award and Faulkner's subsequent acceptance speech at Stockholm, the novelist was honored by his own country with the William Dean Howells Medal of the American Academy of Arts and Letters. The next year, 1951, he received the National Book Award and was recognized with the Ordre National de la Legion D'Honneur by the French consul in New Orleans. He received the National Book Award and a Pulitzer Prize in 1955 for *A Fable*, and in 1963 a Pulitzer Prize for *The Reivers*. Over the years there were other awards.

In Mississippi, Faulkner's activities resembled those of any number of Oxford citizens. He liked to ride horseback and to hunt; he owned a sail boat, which he took out on nearby Sardis Lake. For a brief time he was scoutmaster for a troop of Oxford Boy Scouts. He spent a great deal of time on his farm, and he worked at restoring the ante-bellum mansion which he had purchased. Faulkner and his wife had lost their first child, but the second, a daughter named Jill, was born in 1933, and she was always quite close to her father.

In 1947 Faulkner agreed to confer with some English classes at the University of Mississippi. In recent years he filled the position of writer-in-residence at the University of Virginia, under a grant from the Emily Clark Balch Fund for American Literature.

And he continued to read and to write. His reading, he told classes at the University of Virginia, consisted of old favorites; he said he had nearly stopped reading contemporaries, but yearly turned back to *Don Quixote*, the Old Testament, the works of Shakespeare, *Moby Dick, Madame Bovary*, the novels of Dickens and Conrad, some of Balzac, Chekhov, Gogol, Artzybashev.[12] Although he was not so prolific after the 1930's, he managed to bring out seven more novels and several volumes of short stories before his death. To say there is a noticeable decline in the quality of the works after 1940 is fashionable, but probably critically unsound. His last novel, *The Reivers*, was published June 4, 1962, a little over a month before the novelist died.

Faulkner's retreat to Oxford and his relative seclusion there have been widely commented upon. It is said that he plowed up his driveway so that he would not have to receive visitors. To the community he was an eccentric, sometimes given to alcoholic excess; to the literary world he was an enigma, anti-intellectual, quiet, and reluctant to be thought of as a literary man. Faulkner's typical pose is illustrated in the following comment:

> I'm a countryman. My life is farmland and horses and the raising of grain and feed. I took up writing simply because I liked it—it was something very fine, and so I have no plans—I look after my farm and my horses and then when there is time I write, or if I have something that I want to write, I will find the time to write it, but just to be a writer is not my life; my life is a farmer, so in that sense, I'm not a writer because that doesn't come first. I always find time to do the writing, but I do other things also.[13]

The problems of Faulkner biography are numerous, for Faulkner's own reticence about publicity has significantly multiplied stories about him. Like the telling of a joke, the recounting of a Faulkner tale is changed slightly each time it is told. There are, for example, three versions of the story about Faulkner's reaction to the Nobel Prize: in one, he was drying dishes at a hunting camp; in the second, he was chopping wood, and in the third, he was liming a field, when the news came. According to the first version, he didn't miss a swipe on the dish he was drying when he heard of the award. In versions two and three, he immediately went back to chopping wood or liming the field.

It does seem certain that the novelist was very much aware of the public image he was creating. He liked to emphasize his ruralism and counted among his friends few literary people. In the spring of 1962 he declined the invitation of President and Mrs. John F. Kennedy to a White House dinner honoring America's Nobel Prize winners by commenting, "Why, that's a hundred miles away. That's a long way to go just to eat." Faulkner was at Charlottesville at the time and was the only absentee. His sense of legend and his great story-telling abilities seemingly went beyond the boundaries of Yoknapatawpha County and entered the realms of his own life.

On the other hand, he was not entirely reticent about commenting on his work. As writer-in-residence at the University of Virginia, he not only discussed his works with students, faculty members, and visitors, but allowed the sessions to be recorded, some of which have been published as *Faulkner in the University* (1959). Also, during his seminars in Japan in August, 1955, recordings were made and published as *Faulkner at Nagano* (1956).

Faulkner once said, "I hope to be the only unregimented and unrecorded individual left in the world." The facts of the novelist's life can be told in a handful of pages; the man, the truth about him, may possibly never be reached.

On Friday, July 6, 1962, William Faulkner died. The next day he was buried in the Oxford cemetery and his townsmen honored him by closing their stores, even though it was market day. The placards on their doors and in their windows read:

IN MEMORY
of
WILLIAM FAULKNER
This Business Will Be
CLOSED
From 2:00 to 2:15 P.M.
Today, July 7, 1962

NOTES

1 Frederick L. Gwynn and Joseph L. Blotner, *Faulkner in the University* (Charlottesville, 1959), 249.

2 Virginia O. Bardsley, "William C. Falkner: His Life and Works," unpublished biography in possession of the author.

3 Phil Stone, "William Faulkner: The Man and His Work," *The Oxford Magazine*, I (April, June, November, 1934), 4.

4 Hamilton Basso, "William Faulkner: Man and Writer," *Saturday Review* (July 28, 1962), 33.

5 *Faulkner in the University*, 21.

6 *Ibid.*, 58.

7 Frederick J. Hoffman and Olga W. Vickery (eds.), *William Faulkner: Three Decades of Criticism* (East Lansing, 1960), 82.

8 *Faulkner in the University*, 104.

9 "Introduction," *Sanctuary* (Modern Library Edition, 1932), vii.

10 Robert A. Jelliffe (ed.), *Faulkner at Nagano* (Tokyo, 1956), 9.

11 *Faulkner in the University*, 90.

12 *Ibid.*, 50.

13 *Faulkner at Nagano*, 142.

12

A NOTE ON METHOD

William Faulkner's works cannot be easily categorized. For one thing, there is room for dispute as to which of Faulkner's prose pieces are stories, which are sketches, which should properly be called novellas—and even which of the so-called novels are really novels. Are *The Unvanquished* and *Go Down, Moses* novels or collections of short stories? Each is made up largely of short pieces published earlier as stories. Each also has a unity which is the basis for the claim of many scholars that they are novels.

In preparing the index of characters in this volume, the authors have considered *The Unvanquished* as a novel. In other words, the overall work has been cited, as have *As I Lay Dying, The Sound and the Fury,* and the other novels. Individual stories published earlier and brought into the book have also been cited. But *Go Down, Moses* (published originally under the title *Go Down, Moses and Other Stories*) has been treated differently. The overall work has not been cited. Each of the stories in the collection— those published earlier as well as those published in the book for the first time—have.

The other major collections (*These 13, Doctor Martino and*

13

Other Stories, Knight's Gambit, Collected Stories of William Faulkner, and *Big Woods*) have been given similar treatment in the index of characters: the collection itself is not cited; the individual stories are. An exception was made in the case of *Big Woods.* Each story has an italicized prelude which is not a part of the story itself, and in citing the few characters in these, *Big Woods* was used.

Miss Zilphia Gant and *Idyll in the Desert,* though they were published in book form, have been considered as short stories. So have the sixteen short fictional pieces published in the New Orleans *Times-Picayune* in 1925 and brought together in the 1958 volume edited by Carvel Collins as *New Orleans Sketches.* The long story or short novel titled "Old Man" has not been individually cited as a reference in the character index because it originally appeared published jointly with "Wild Palms" under a single title, *The Wild Palms.* Thus, characters from both pieces are listed as from *The Wild Palms.*

Many of Faulkner's stories were revised and incorporated into longer works. Some were incorporated into other stories. Titles were changed. "That Evening Sun" was originally "That Evening Sun Go Down." "Turn About" became "Turnabout." The story "The Unvanquished" became, after revision, the "Riposte in Tertio" section of *The Unvanquished.*

It is obvious, then, that the list of Faulkner's works will vary somewhat from scholar to scholar. The list at the back of this volume is not intended to be the definitive one, which it is not, but merely the most useful one for the purposes of this book. For those who would like to go further into the matter of Faulkner bibliography, the authors recommend James B. Meriwether's *The Literary Career of William Faulkner: A Bibliographical Study* (Princeton, 1961). The reference used for locating the stories as first published has been Professor Meriwether's "William Faulkner: A Check List," *Princeton University Library Chronicle,* XVIII (Spring, 1957), 136–58.

INDEX OF CHARACTERS

Ad, a camp cook for Major Cassius de Spain. "Lion."

Adams, mayor of Jefferson. He was succeeded by Manfred de Spain. *The Town.*

Addie. *See* Bundren, Addie.

Ailanthia, the grandmother of Elly. She was killed when her granddaughter deliberately wrecked the car in which they were riding. "Elly."

Akers, a coon-hunter who stumbled over one of Thomas Sutpen's "wild Negroes" sent into the swamp to drive out game. *Absalom, Absalom!*

Alabama Red. *See* Red.

Albert, an employee in Moseley's drug store in Mottstown, where Dewey Dell Bundren first went to buy abortion pills. *As I Lay Dying.*

Alford, Dr., a practicing physician in Jefferson. This young doctor, at the insistence of Miss Jenny (Virginia Sartoris Du Pre), treated Colonel Bayard Sartoris. *Sartoris, As I Lay Dying.*

Alice, the Negro cook at Miss Ballenbaugh's hunting camp between Jefferson and Memphis. *The Reivers.*

Allanova, Myra, the proprietor of an exclusive New York shop dealing in ties. "A short dumpy woman" with handsome dark eyes, she presented V. K. Ratliff with his first sophisticated tie, one tinted peach "like the back of a sunburned gal." *The Mansion.*

Allen, Bobbie, a waitress in a Jefferson restaurant of low repute. Over thirty, she initiated Joe Christmas into the rites of sex when he was eighteen and refused to believe him when he confessed that he might have some "nigger blood." After McEachern's murder, she refused to marry Christmas and run away with him. *Light in August.*

Allison, Howard (1866–   ), a Republican federal judge in Mississippi. He was married in 1894, and his only son, Howard, was killed in 1913 at age ten. "Beyond."

Allison, Howard (1903–13), ten-year-old son of a Republican federal judge in Mississippi. He was killed in 1913. "Beyond."

Ames, Dalton, one of the lovers of Candace Compson. Candace's brother Quentin threatened to kill Ames and tried to beat him up, but he failed at both. *The Sound and the Fury.*

Angelique, an old blind woman. She could not be fooled like people with sight who had "nothing to do but believe everything they look at." According to her, the Corporal was an "anarchist who is murdering Frenchmen." *A Fable.*

Anse, the marshal of a small town near Boston. He arrested Quentin Compson for kidnapping. *The Sound and the Fury.*

Anse. *See* Bundren, Anse.

Anse (Old Man). *See* Holland, Anselm.

Antonio, a middle-aged Sicilian restaurant owner in the French Quarter of New Orleans. Pathologically jealous of his wife's affections, he murdered his innocent employee. "Jealousy."

Armstid, Henry, a Mississippi-born farmer. Father of four, he lived in the Frenchman's Bend region near the Bundren home with his wife Lula (Martha, according to *Light in August*). He and his wife befriended Lena Grove, and the Bundren family, and were swindled by Flem Snopes in two major business deals. Henry ended his days in the Jackson asylum. *As I Lay Dying.*

Light in August, The Hamlet, The Town, The Mansion, "Spotted Horses," "Lizards in Jamshyd's Courtyard," "Shingles for the Lord."

Atkins, Miss, the dietitian in a Memphis orphanage. Twenty-seven years old, she was "old enough to have to take a few amorous risks but still young enough to attach a great deal of importance not so much to love, but to being caught at it." She was "caught at it" by innocent five-year-old Joe Christmas and was determined to get him sent to the "nigger orphanage." *Light in August.*

Aunt Callie. *See* Nelson, Caroline.

Aunt Jenny. *See* Du Pre, Virginia Sartoris.

Ayers, Major, a frequently naïve and confused British army officer. He was primarily interested in a money-making scheme, one based on a cure for constipation. *Mosquitoes.*

Ayers, Freddie, a British first mate of a filthy ship, the "Diana." By mistake, he killed the ship's mess boy, Yo Ho. "Yo Ho and Two Bottles of Rum."

B

Backhouse, Melisandre, Mrs., the granddaughter of Rosa Millard, and a native of Memphis. She married Philip St.-Just Backhouse during the Civil War. "My Grandmother Millard."

Backhouse, Philip St.-Just, a Confederate officer from Tennessee. He married Melisandre Backhouse. "My Grandmother Millard."

Backus, owner of a decaying plantation near Jefferson. Father of Melisandre Harriss Stevens, he died shortly after his daughter's first marriage, having waited long enough "to make sure his son-in-law was actually a czar or anyway the empire a going and solvent one. . . ." *The Mansion.*

Backus, Melisandre. *See* Stevens, Melisandre Backus Harriss.

Baddrington, Harold (Plex), a World War II buddy of Charles (Chick) Mallison. *The Mansion.*

Baird, Dr., a specialist from Atlanta who was called in to treat the dying Donald Mahon. *Soldiers' Pay.*

Baker, Joe. *See* Jobaker.

Ballenbaugh, Miss, a "fifty-year-old maiden" who owned a small farm and store near a river crossing between Jefferson and Memphis. "Prim fleshless severe," she kept clean accommodations for fox- and coon-hunters. *The Reivers.*

Ballenbaugh, Boyd, brother of Tyler Ballenbaugh. He murdered Lonnie Grinnup, then went to his brother and demanded ten dollars for doing a job he had not been asked to do. "Hand Upon the Waters."

Ballenbaugh, Tyler, a farmer of Yoknapatawpha County, brother of Boyd. He took out a $5,000 insurance policy on Lonnie Grinnup. "Hand Upon the Waters."

Ballott, Mr., the foreman at Maury Priest's livery stable in Jefferson. *The Reivers.*

Barbour, a Sunday-school teacher in Jefferson. "Uncle Willy."

Barger, Sonny, a storekeeper in "Nigger Row" where Uncle Willy Christian bought bootleg whiskey. "Uncle Willy."

Barron, Homer, a Northerner and day laborer in Jefferson. He courted Miss Emily Grierson, but because he was not the marrying kind, she poisoned him. "A Rose for Emily."

Bascomb, Maury L., the "handsome flashing swaggering worthless brother" of Carolyn Bascomb Compson. He borrowed money from almost anyone, even Dilsey. His activities included an affair with Mrs. Patterson. *The Sound and the Fury.*

Basket, Herman, an Indian. He grew up with Ikkemotubbe and Craw-Ford. David Hogganbeck courted his sister. "A Justice."

Basket, John, the Indian to whom V. K. Ratliff sent Lucius Hogganbeck for a hiccough cure. "A Bear Hunt."

Basket, Three, one of Issetibbeha's chief counselors. He wore an enameled snuffbox through one ear. *Big Woods,* "Red Leaves."

Beale, Colonel, a British officer convinced he saw the Corporal slain in 1914. *A Fable.*

Beard, Mrs., the owner of a Jefferson boarding house. She was kind to Lena Grove when that very pregnant girl arrived in town searching for Lucas Burch. *Sartoris, Light in August.*

Beard, Virgil, the son of gristmill owner W. C. Beard. Young Virgil copied Byron Snopes's anonymous letters to Narcissa Benbow. A prized possession of his was a pistol that "projected a stream of ammoniac water excruciatingly painful to the eyes." *Sartoris.*

Beard, W. C., father of Virgil. He owned a gristmill. *Sartoris.*

Beauchamp, Bobo, "another motherless Beauchamp child," a grandson of Tennie's Jim, known familiarly as a "cousin" of Lucas Beauchamp, "a McCaslin too." He was the pivotal character in the horse-automobile trade involving Lucius Priest, Boon Hogganbeck, and Ned during their escapade in and near Memphis. *The Reivers.*

Beauchamp, Henry (1898–   ), the son of Lucas and Molly Beauchamp, and foster-brother of Carothers Edmonds. Raised together, the two were inseparable until "haughty ancestral pride" descended on young Edmonds. His rebuff of Henry was met with quiet dignity. "The Fire and the Hearth."

Beauchamp, Hubert Fitz-Hubert, the bachelor-owner of "Warwick," a plantation near Yoknapatawpha County. After several ineffectual attempts, he finally succeeded in marrying off his sister, Sophonsiba, to Theophilus McCaslin. One of his Negro slaves, Tennie, took his surname and passed it on to her children. "A bluff burly roaring childlike man," he was the godfather of Isaac McCaslin. "Was," "The Bear."

Beauchamp, James Thucydus (December 29, 1864—?), the fourth child of Tennie Beauchamp and Tomey's Turl. For some years he was regular help in the de Spain-Edmonds hunting parties, until he vanished December 29, 1885. He was traced to Tennessee so that he could be given his share of the L. Q. Carothers McCaslin legacy, and there lost. His granddaughter bore Carothers (Roth) Edmonds' bastard son. *Big Woods,* "The Bear," "The Old People," "Delta Autumn."

Beauchamp, Lucas Quintus McCaslin (March 17, 1874–   ), the son of Tennie Beauchamp and Tomey's Turl, and grandson of Lucius Q. C. McCaslin and Negress Tomasina. A proud man (I ain't a Edmonds . . . I belong to the old lot. I'm a McCaslin."), he lived with his wife Molly on a ten-acre lot seventeen miles from Jefferson. It had been deeded to him and his heirs by Zachary (Zack) Edmonds, a man whom he had nearly killed years earlier. In his late middle years, he was accused of the murder of Vinson Gowrie and was saved through the heroic efforts of two boys, Charles (Chick) Mallison and Aleck Sander, and an old maid, Miss Habersham. *Intruder in the Dust, The Reivers,* "The Fire and the Hearth," "Pantaloon in Black," "The Bear," "Gold Is Not Always," "A Point of Law."

Beauchamp, Molly (Mollie), the wife of Lucas Beauchamp, grandmother of Samuel Worsham Beauchamp, sister of Hamp Worsham. She was the daughter of one of old Dr. Habersham's slaves. "A tiny, doll-sized woman" with a mind of her own, she nursed Carothers Edmonds for the first six months of his life, forcing Lucas to face Zachary Edmonds, the baby's father, and demand the return of his wife. Forty-five years later she instituted divorce proceedings against Lucas and dropped them only after he agreed to abandon a money-divining machine. *Intruder in the Dust*, "The Fire and the Hearth," "Go Down, Moses."

Beauchamp, Nat. *See* Wilkins, Nat Beauchamp.

Beauchamp, Philip Manigault, an American soldier in World War I. With Buchwald and the Iowan he volunteered, on the basis of a three-day pass to Paris, for a mission which turned out to be the assassination of General Gragnon. Beauchamp supported the general as Buchwald shot him. *A Fable.*

Beauchamp, Samuel Worsham, the grandson of Molly and Lucas Beauchamp, orphaned at birth by the death of his mother and desertion of his father. Involved in the numbers racket, he was executed in Joliet, Illinois when he was twenty-six for killing a policeman. His body was returned to Jefferson through the assistance of Gavin Stevens. "Go Down, Moses."

Beauchamp, Tennie (1838—?), a Negro slave, won by Amodeus McCaslin from Hubert Beauchamp in 1859 in a poker game. She married Tomey's Turl (Terrel) in the same year, and they were the parents of six children. "The Bear," "Was," "The Fire and the Hearth."

Bedenberry, Brother, a Negro lay minister from the area near Jefferson. He was almost snatched out of his pulpit by the fleeing Joe Christmas. *Light in August.*

Ben. *See* Old Ben.

Benbow, Judge, a Jefferson jurist. He appointed himself executor of Goodhue Coldfield's estate and handled the matter of Judith Sutpen's headstone in 1884. *Absalom, Absalom!, The Unvanquished, The Hamlet.*

Benbow, Belle Mitchell, the wife of Horace Benbow, divorced wife of Harry Mitchell, and mother of Little Belle. Of her Benbow remarked, "When you marry somebody else's wife, you start off maybe ten years behind, from somebody else's scratch and scratching." When he left her, after ten years of marriage, she returned to her father's home in Kentucky, but came back after Benbow's defeat at the Goodwin trial. *Sartoris, Sanctuary.*

Benbow, Cassius Q., a Negro carriage driver for the Benbows. He ran off with the Yankees during the Civil War, returned to Jefferson to run for marshal, and was defeated because of Colonel John Sartoris' voting restrictions. *The Unvanquished,* "Skirmish at Sartoris."

Benbow, Horace (1886–   ), a Jefferson-born lawyer. The son of Will and Julia Benbow, brother of Narcissa Benbow Sartoris, he was educated at Sewanee and Oxford. In 1919 he married Mrs. Belle Mitchell, a divorcee, and moved from Jefferson to Kinston. Ten years later he found himself "mixed up with moonshiners and streetwalkers" after he had left his wife because he could no longer stand to carry a package of dripping shrimp home to her every Friday. He considered his defense of accused murderer Lee Goodwin (which proved unsuccessful because of Temple Drake's perjury) something for which his soul had been serving "an apprenticeship" for forty-three years. *Sartoris, Sanctuary.*

Benbow, Narcissa. *See* Sartoris, Narcissa Benbow.

Benbow, Percy, the son of Judge Benbow. After his father's death, he opened the private Goodhue Coldfield portfolio to find the record of how much the judge had deposited in Rosa Coldfield's account, money secretly earned by bets at a Memphis racetrack. *Absalom, Absalom!*

Benjy. *See* Compson, Benjamin.

Berry, Louis, an Indian. He was a friend of Three Basket and one of Issetibbeha's chief counselors. "Red Leaves."

Best, Henry, a Jefferson alderman. He helped investigate the brass works theft by Flem Snopes. *The Town.*

Bidet, General, a group commander in the French army during World War I. The only child of the daughter of a retired sergeant-major of marines and a Savoyard schoolmaster, Bidet, a "short, healthy, pot-bellied little man" of fifty, declared that "no army was better than its anus." In his profession, all that remained for him to achieve was his marshal's baton. *A Fable.*

Bidwell, a storekeeper in Division, Mississippi, who knew Henry (Hawkshaw) Stribling's past. "Hair."

Biglin, Luther, a Mississippi countryman. "A half farmer, half dog trainer, half market hunter," he was the best shot in the county. As jailer during Ephraim Bishop's tenure as sheriff, a period coinciding with Mink Snopes's release from prison, he also acted as bodyguard to Flem Snopes, although Flem was not aware of this. Biglin slept only from seven to half-past nine in the evening, and it was during these hours that Mink succeeded in shooting Flem, almost as though he had "done it outen pure and simple spite." *The Mansion.*

Binford, Dewitt (Dee-wit), a Frenchman's Bend resident. He married one of the Snopes girls and agreed to take care of Byron Snopes's four "Indians." *The Town,* "The Waifs."

Binford, Lucius, the long-mourned dead lover of and one-time pimp for Reba Rivers. During his life he acted as "landlord" for her house of prostitution in Memphis. His only weakness was horse racing. *Sanctuary, The Mansion, The Reivers.*

Birdsong, the white night watchman at the Jefferson sawmill. His throat was cut "clean to the neckbone" by the crazed, grief-stricken Rider. "Pantaloon in Black."

Birdsong, Preacher, a crony of Matt Levitt. They shared an interest in boxing. *The Town.*

Bishop, Elma, wife of Ephriam and his office deputy. *The Town.*

Bishop, Ephriam, sheriff of Jefferson who alternated terms of office with Hub Hampton. He felt responsible for the defense and protection of human life in Jefferson, "even when the human life was Flem Snopes's." *The Mansion.*

Black, a taxi driver who helped acquaint the flying acrobats with the town officials. "Death Drag."

Blair, Harrison, a banker and horseman. Wealthy from his wife's Oklahoma oil, he spent most of his time and money on pedigreed horses. "Fox Hunt."

Blair, John, a poverty-stricken poet. He repaid the charity of his host, Roger Howes, by falling in love with Mrs. Howes. "Artist at Home."

Bland, a graduate of Yale and a Rhodes scholar at Oxford. He became a member of the Royal Flying Corps during World War I and was a friend of the twins, Bayard and John Sartoris. "Ad Astra."

Bland, Mrs., a "remarkably preserved" Kentucky matron, mother of

Gerald, her "Harvard boy." It was rumored she was grooming him "to seduce a duchess sometime." *The Sound and the Fury.*

Bland, Gerald, a native of Kentucky and acquaintance of Quentin Compson at Harvard. He gave Quentin a black eye. *The Sound and the Fury.*

Bogard, H. S., a captain in the Royal Flying Corps during World War I. He befriended Claude Hope. "Turnabout."

Bolivar, Uncle Dick, a shriveled old man who made and sold nostrums and charms. He used a divining rod to help discover buried money on the Old Frenchman Place. "Lizards in Jamshyd's Courtyard."

Bon, Charles (1829, according to "Chronology"; December, 1831 or January, 1832, according to *Absalom, Absalom!*—May 3, 1865), the New Orleans-born unacknowledged son of Thomas Sutpen and Eulalia Bon Sutpen. He was "a young man of worldly elegance and assurance beyond his years." After a brief time at the University of Mississippi, he served gallantly as a lieutenant in the University Greys, C.S.A., only to be murdered by Henry Sutpen on his return to Sutpen's Hundred to claim his bride-to-be, his half-sister, Judith Sutpen. *Absalom, Absalom!*

Bon, Charles Etienne Saint-Valery (de Saint Velery), New Orleans-born son of Charles Bon and an octoroon mistress. Reared by Clytie and Judith Sutpen, this "strange lonely boy . . . with his four names and his sixteenth-part black blood" married (in 1879, according to "Genealogy"; in *ca.* 1881, according to *Absalom, Absalom!*) a full blooded Negress, and cursed his heritage and the world until his death (from yellow fever, according to *Absalom, Absalom!*; from smallpox, according to "Chronology") at Sutpen's Hundred. *Absalom, Absalom!*

Bon, Eulalia. *See* Sutpen, Eulalia.

Bond, Jim (1882, according to "Genealogy"; 1881 or 1882, according to *Absalom, Absalom!*—   ), the mulatto son of Charles Etienne de Saint Velery Bon and a full-blooded Negress. The only living descendant of Thomas Sutpen, this "hulking slack-mouthed saddle-colored boy," a mentally deficient white Negro, disappeared from Yoknapatawpha County in 1910 after the burning of the Sutpen mansion. *Absalom, Absalom!*

Bonds, Jack, a member of the Provine gang. "A Bear Hunt."

Bookwright, Calvin, a Frenchman's Bend distiller of potent corn whiskey. *The Mansion.*

Bookwright, Herman, one of several young men who left Frenchman's Bend "suddenly overnight" following the "hors-de-combat creek-bridge evening" involving Eula Varner and Hoake McCarron. *The Mansion.*

Bookwright, Homer, a Frenchman's Bend resident. He was supposed to help re-shingle Reverend Whitfield's church. *The Mansion,* "Shingles for the Lord."

Bookwright, Odum, a well-to-do farmer and resident of Frenchman's Bend. He was a friend of V. K. Ratliff and co-purchaser with Ratliff and Henry Armstid of the Old Frenchman Place from Flem Snopes. When Bookwright's seventeen-year-old daughter tried to elope with Buck Thorpe, Bookwright killed Thorpe and was tried for murder. *The Hamlet, The Mansion,* "Tomorrow."

Bowden, Matt, a Reconstruction opportunist. He formed a dangerous alliance with Ab Snopes and Major Grumby. Harassed by Bayard Sartoris' efforts to avenge the murder of Granny Rosa Millard, he betrayed both Snopes and Grumby; he was also responsible for shooting Amodeus McCaslin in the arm. He was last seen on his way to Texas. *The Unvanquished.*

Boyd, Mrs., mother of Howard Boyd. "The Brooch."

Boyd, Amy, wife of Howard Boyd. "The Brooch."

Boyd, Howard, the only child of widowed, stroke-ridden Mrs. Boyd. He attended the University of Virginia, married an unfaithful girl named Amy, and committed suicide because he could not live with either his mother or his wife, nor could he live without them. "The Brooch."

Bradley, Mr. and Mrs., temporary Wisconsin neighbors of Harry Wilbourne and Charlotte Rittenmeyer. *The Wild Palms.*

Breckbridge, Gavin, Drusilla Hawk Sartoris' fiancé before his death at Shiloh. He gave the horse, Bobolink, to Drusilla. *The Unvanquished,* "Skirmish at Sartoris," "Raid."

Breton. *See* Paul.

Bridesman, Captain, an RAF flight commander during World War I. He was assigned the special task of escorting the defecting German general to the Allied aerodrome. *A Fable.*

Bridger, the partner in violence of Matt Bowden. *The Unvanquished.*

Briggins, Lycurgus, grandson of Uncle Parsham Hood and son of Mary. A perceptive young Negro, he was of considerable help to the Hogganbeck-Ned-Lucius Priest trio. *The Reivers.*

Broussard, owner and manager of a New Orleans restaurant. *Mosquitoes.*

Brown, Joe. *See* Burch, Lucas.

Brownlee, Percival (1830–   ), a Negro slave "bookepper." He was bought by Theophilus McCaslin from N. B. Forrest on March 3, 1856, for $265. Brownlee, "who couldn't keep books and couldn't farm either," tried conducting revival meetings, and later became the proprietor of a select New Orleans brothel. "The Bear."

Brummage, Judge, the Jefferson jurist who sentenced Mink Snopes to life imprisonment for the murder of Jack Houston. *The Mansion.*

Buchwald, an American private during World War I. His grandfather had been rabbi of a Minsk synagogue, and his father was a Brooklyn tailor. Within two years after passage of the prohibition law he had become "czar of a million-dollar empire covering the entire Atlantic coast." He was, in France, assigned with Beauchamp and the Iowan the task of assassinating General Gragnon. *A Fable.*

Buckner, "Buck" and "Billie," a married couple. The husband managed the defunct Utah mine to which Harry Wilbourne and Charlotte Rittenmeyer fled, and the wife survived an abortion performed by Wilbourne. *The Wild Palms.*

Buffaloe, the Jefferson city electrician, "a dreamy myopic gentian-eyed mechanical wizard." In 1904 he drove the town's first automobile and frightened Colonel Bayard Sartoris' matched team, an incident which resulted in the passing of an "edict that no gasoline-propelled vehicle should ever operate on the streets of Jefferson." *The Town, The Reivers.*

Buford, a deputy sheriff of Jefferson. A staunch supporter of Sheriff Kennedy, "he looked like a spaniel waiting to be told to spring into the water." *Light in August.*

Bunch, Byron, a Jefferson resident who spent "six days of every week for seven years at the planing mill, feeding boards into the machinery." His only social intercourse had been restricted to directing a country church choir and evening talks with the renegade Reverend Hightower until the arrival in Jefferson of Lena Grove, for whom he "got himself desperated up to risking all." For Lena he abandoned the philosophy by which he had governed his life: "a fellow is more afraid of the trouble he might have than he ever is of the trouble he's already got." *Light in August.*

Bundren, Addie, reluctant wife for over thirty years of Anse Bundren. Mother of five children, one of whom was illegitimate, she believed that life in the world she knew "was terrible" and that death "was the answer to it." When death came, the Bundrens were bound by a promise to carry her body home to Jefferson. *As I Lay Dying.*

Bundren, Anse, a lazy "redneck" Yoknapatawpha farmer. Husband of the dying Addie, father of four, a man who "does everything like he is hoping all the time he really can't do it and can quit trying to," he achieved his goals at the end of the burial journey: buried Addie near her family in Jefferson, got new teeth with Dewey Dell Bundren's abortion money, and married a new wife. *As I Lay Dying.*

Bundren, Cash, a carpenter, eldest child of Anse and Addie. He believed it "better to build a tight chicken coop than a shoddy courthouse." When he fell from a church roof, he estimated the fall at "twenty-eight foot, four and a half inches, about." *As I Lay Dying.*

Bundren, Darl, the second child of Anse and Addie, considered "the queer one." He recognized intuitively that "the safe things are not always the best things." After the burial journey, he was committed to the state asylum at Jackson. *As I Lay Dying,* "Uncle Willy."

Bundren, Dewey Dell, the only daughter of Anse and Addie, she carried within her on the burial journey the somewhat casually conceived offspring of Lafe, a neighbor. She was seventeen years old. *The Sound and the Fury, As I Lay Dying.*

Bundren, Jewel, the illegitimate son of Addie Bundren and the Reverend Whitfield. This hard-working, tough-minded man had but two passionate interests: his mother, whom he would save "from the water and from the fire," and his horse. *As I Lay Dying.*

Bundren, Vardaman, the last child of Anse and Addie. Too young to grasp the meaning of death, this lost, confused youngster linked his mother with a fish. *As I Lay Dying.*

Burch, Lucas, a brash hand for "playing jokes on folks." In flight from Lena Grove and responsibility, this "weakly handsome" braggart assumed the name of Brown and worked briefly at the Jefferson planing mill, for "there was not even enough left of him to do a good, shrewd job of shirking." He shared a cabin with Joe Christmas, engaged in bootlegging, informed on Christmas, deserted Lena a second time, frantically defended himself in rat-like fashion from Byron Bunch, and escaped on a passing train. *Light in August.*

Burchett, a family who took care of orphaned Susan Reed. Kind and naïve, Mr. and Mrs. Burchett never realized what a strange girl they had taken in. "Hair."

Burden, Calvin (–1874), the youngest child of Nathaniel (Burrington) Burden. At twelve he ran away to sea, and later turned Catholic and lived for a year in a monastery. Ten years later he reached Missouri from the west, married, repudiated the Catholic Church, saying he "would not belong to a church full of frog-eating slaveholders," and began to indoctrinate his son, Nathaniel, II, with "hellfire and brimstone" dogma. He taught his son and three daughters to hate two things: hell and slaveholders. He and his grandson, Calvin, II, were shot by Colonel John Sartoris in the street in Jefferson in 1874 as they tried to protect Negro voting rights. *Light in August, The Unvanquished.*

Burden, Calvin, II (1854–74), the only son of Nathaniel, II, and Juana Burden. He was ringbearer, at age twelve, at the wedding of his parents. He and his grandfather, Calvin Burden, accused of "stirring up the Negroes," were killed by two shots from the same pistol, fired by Colonel John Sartoris. *Light in August, The Unvanquished,* "Skirmish at Sartoris."

Burden, Joanna (*ca.* 1888–1939), a Mississippi-born spinster of New England forebears. The daughter by his second wife of Nathaniel Burden, and granddaughter of Calvin Burden, she inherited her father's rabid anti-Catholicism and stolid Calvinist religious beliefs and her grandfather's antislavery fanaticism. Unable to forget the murder of her half-brother, Calvin, II, in 1874, over a question of Negro voting, she devoted nearly forty years of her life to giving religious, financial, and business advice to those concerned with Negro schools and colleges in the South. After the arrival of Joe Christmas, who lived in a shack on her property, she devoted herself to him, as avid lover and adviser, looking on him as a symbol of her responsibility, a member "of a race doomed and cursed to be forever and ever a part of the white race's doom and curse for its sins." Her frantic efforts to force Joe to "admit" his race and to kneel with her in prayer brought about her savage murder. *Light in August.*

Burden, Juana, first wife of Nathaniel Burden, II, and mother of Calvin Burden, II. She was Spanish. *Light in August.*

Burden, Nathaniel, a minister, the progenitor of the family. His name originally was Burrington. He had ten children, the youngest of whom was Calvin. *Light in August.*

Burden, Nathaniel, II (1836—?), the only son of Calvin, born in St. Louis. When fourteen, he ran away to the west, returning sixteen years later with a Spanish woman, Juana, and a nearly twelve-year-old son, Calvin, II. He had come home to get married because there were only priests where he had been living. In 1866 he and his father were granted a commission from the federal government to help the freed Negroes, and the move to Jefferson from Kansas was made. After his father and his son were shot down in 1874, and following the death of his wife, he married a second time, to a New Hampshire woman sent down by a cousin of his. To them, in 1888, a daughter was born, named Joanna, after Calvin's mother. *Light in August*

Burgess, a Jefferson resident. When Benjy Compson took chase after his daughter, Burgess knocked Benjy out with a fence picket. *The Sound and the Fury.*

Burney, Mr. and Mrs., a Charlestown, Georgia couple who lost their son Dewey in World War I, and in so doing gained a much-desired prestige. Dewey had enlisted because he was under indictment for stealing fifty pounds of sugar. *Soldiers' Pay.*

Butch, a "hulking youth" of Jefferson, eager to lynch Will Mayes for the supposed rape of Minnie Cooper. "Dry September."

C

Caddy. *See* Compson, Candace.

Cain, the owner of the country store where Ab Snopes was supposed to buy the separator for his wife. *The Hamlet.*

Cajun (Cajan), The, an alligator trapper in the Louisiana bayous. He took for a brief time the Tall Convict as a partner until the rising river forced them to abandon their site. *The Wild Palms.*

Caldwell, Sam, a flagman for the railroad. A close friend of Miss Corrie and Reba Rivers, he proved to be an equally staunch help to Boon Hogganbeck, Ned, and Lucius Priest throughout the complex matter of the horse-automobile swap and horse races. *The Reivers.*

Callaghan, a stable owner who tried to teach Mrs. Harrison Blair how to ride. "Fox Hunt."

Callaghan, Miss, a schoolteacher in Jefferson. "Uncle Willy."

Callicoat, David. *See* Ikkemotubbe.

Callie, Aunt, the nurse-mammy of the young sons of Maury Priest of Jefferson. *The Reivers.*

Captain, The, captain of a lugger used by Joe, the bootlegger, to haul whiskey. "Once Aboard the Lugger."

Carl, a ship's steward, and friend of George. "Divorce in Naples."

Carter, an architect, Wilfred Midgleston's boss. "Black Music."

Caspey. *See* Strother, Caspey.

Cayley, Hence, a young girl courted simultaneously by Max Harriss and Sebastian Gualdres. She dismissed them both, also simultaneously. "Knight's Gambit."

Charley, a young intern from the county hospital whose amorous activities with Miss Atkins were overheard by young Joe Christmas. *Light in August.*

Charlie, one of Candace Compson's beaux. Her brother Benjy tried to separate the pair as they embraced on the porch swing. *The Sound and the Fury.*

Chick. *See* Mallison, Charles.

Chlory, a Negress, servant of Judge Allison. "Beyond."

Christian, Walter, a Negro employee of Uncle Willy Christian's. "His grandfather had belonged to Uncle Willy's grandfather before the surrender." *The Town.*

Christian, Uncle Willy, a one-hundred-ten pound Jefferson dope addict. Uncle Willy ran the drugstore which his father had established, successfully resisted the efforts of Jefferson do-gooders to "cure" him, and died when his own $1,500 plane crashed. When he was sixty, he married a Memphis whore. "Even women couldn't beat him, because in spite of them he wound up his life getting fun out of being alive and he died doing the thing that was the most fun of all." Gavin Stevens entertained Linda Snopes Kohl in his drugstore. *The Town, The Mansion,* "Uncle Willy."

Christmas, Joe (1894?–1939?), the illegitimate son of Milly Hines, who died at his birth, and a Mexican (?) circus hand, who was murdered by Milly's father, Eupheus Hines. Left in a Memphis orphanage on Christmas Eve, he was adopted when he was five by religious fanatics, Mr. and Mrs. McEachern. He fled from them when he was eighteen, after killing his foster father. Following nearly fifteen years of lonely wandering, he returned to Jefferson, worked at the planing mill, lived in a cabin on the Joanna Burden property, became her lover and doom, destroyed her and defied "his black blood for the last time" by escaping, but was finally captured, brutally mutilated and killed by Percy Grimm. *Light in August.*

Cinthy, the old Negro mammy of Gail Hightower. She and Gail's father related conflicting tales of Grandfather Hightower's fighting in the Civil War. Their stories were in accord on only one point: "grandfather wore no sword" and therefore did not gallop with his sword "waving in front of the rest of them." *Light in August.*

Clapp, Walter, the horse trainer for Colonel Linscomb, near Memphis. *The Reivers.*

Clytie. *See* Sutpen, Clytemnestra.

Cofer, a real estate agent near New Orleans. He rented a Gulf Coast cabin to Harry Wilbourne and Charlotte Rittenmeyer. *The Wild Palms.*

Colbert, David, "Chief man" of all the Chickasaws in the Yoknapatawpha area. "A Courtship."

Coldfield, Miss, a spinster aunt who, after the death in childbirth of Goodhue Coldfield's wife, helped rear Rosa Coldfield, helped arrange the wedding of Ellen Coldfield and Thomas Sutpen, and before 1855 climbed out a window of the Coldfield home and vanished forever. *Absalom, Absalom!*

Coldfield, Ellen. *See* Sutpen, Ellen Coldfield.

Coldfield, Goodhue (–1864), Tennessee-born merchant who moved to Jefferson in 1828. Father of Ellen Coldfield Sutpen and Rosa Coldfield, he lost his wife in childbirth in 1845. An unusually mild-mannered individual, he was stirred from his ordinary quiet isolation by two events: the courtship of Ellen by Thomas Sutpen, and the Civil War. To the first he submitted under pressure; to the second he expressed his bitter hatred by closing his shop, locking himself in his attic, and starving to death. *Absalom, Absalom!*

Coldfield, Rosa (1845–1910), Jefferson-born spinster, daughter of Goodhue Coldfield, sister-in-law of Thomas Sutpen. Almost engaged to the "demon" Sutpen in 1866, she was filled with an "impotent yet indomitable frustration," fostered by her awareness of the frailty of self, her forebearers, and the South. Not believing in the fashionable thesis that mistakes are repaired "by turning your back on them and running," she forced the young man Quentin Compson to listen as she revealed the final horrifying chapter of the downfall of the Sutpen dream. *Absalom, Absalom!*

Compson, Benjamin (Benjy) (April 7, 1895—*ca.* 1936), an idiot, the youngest son of Jason Lycurgus Compson, III, and Carolyn Bascomb Compson. He was twice christened, first Maury, after his mother's brother, and second, Benjamin. Benjy loved three things: his pasture, his sister Candace, and firelight. Castrated in 1913, he was committed to the state asylum in Jackson in 1933 (according to *The Sound and the Fury*); his commitment "didn't stick" and he was returned home, "where sure enough in less than two years he not only burned himself but completely destroyed the house too" (according to *The Mansion*). *See* Idiot. *The Sound and the Fury, The Mansion.*

Compson, Candace (Caddy) (1892–), daughter of Jason Lycurgus Compson, III, and Carolyn Bascomb Compson, mother of Quentin Compson (female), and sister beloved by brother Benjy, envied and detested by brother Jason, and perversely adored by brother Quentin. Her checkered career included affairs with Dalton Ames and with others; pregnancy; a hurried marriage to Indiana banker Sydney Herbert Head on April 25, 1910, ending in divorce in 1911; marriage in 1920 to a minor movie magnate, and divorce by mutual agreement in 1925; and a shadowy period in Paris consorting with Nazi officers during the German occupation in 1940. *The Sound and the Fury, The Mansion,* "That Evening Sun," "A Justice."

Compson, Carolyn Bascomb (–1933), wife of Jason Lycurgus Compson, III, and mother of four children. She spent most of her adult life struggling to understand her children, complaining of her lot, and witnessing the gradual destruction of the family she had married into. *The Sound and the Fury, The Mansion,* "That Evening Sun."

Compson, Charles Stuart, a soldier left for dead in a Georgia swamp by his British regiment. He fashioned himself a wooden leg and overtook his father, Quentin MacLachan Compson, and his son, Jason Lycurgus Compson, at Harrodsburg, Kentucky. He wanted to be a schoolteacher, but became a gambler instead. He gambled wrong when he joined a movement designed to annex the Mississippi Valley to Spain. Because of his own loud talk, his co-plotters arranged to have him evicted from the United States. *The Sound and the Fury.*

Compson, "Damuddy," the grandmother whose death further complicated the lives of the Compson family. *The Sound and the Fury.*

Compson, Jason Lycurgus, son of Charles Stuart Compson and father of Governor Quentin MacLachan Compson. In 1811 he arrived in Yoknapatawpha County, became the Chickasaw agent's clerk within six months and his partner within a year. He traded his little mare to Ikkemotubbe for a solid square mile of land (known successively as the Compson Domain, the Old Governor's, and the Old Compson Place) which later became the center of Jefferson. *The Sound and the Fury, Requiem for a Nun.*

Compson, Jason Lycurgus, II (–1900), a brigade commander in 1865. He failed at Shiloh in 1862, and again at Resaca in

1864. An irresponsible man, he was wont to shoot sweet potatoes off the heads of Negro children, and he put the first mortgage on the Compson land in 1866. He was a member of the Cassius de Spain hunting parties and died in 1900 at the camp in the Tallahatchie River bottom. *The Sound and the Fury, The Town,* "Skirmish at Sartoris," "The Bear," "The Old People," "Delta Autumn," "My Grandmother Millard."

Compson, Mrs. Jason Lycurgus, II, wife of the Brigadier. This friend of Granny Rosa Millard's loaned her some clothing during the skirmish with Federal troops and offered refuge to Bayard Sartoris and Ringo. *The Unvanquished,* "Vendée," "Skirmish at Sartoris," "My Grandmother Millard," "Retreat," "Raid."

Compson, Jason Richmond Lycurgus, III, Jefferson-born lawyer and dipsomaniac. The son of General Jason Lycurgus Compson, II, he married Carolyn Bascomb, fathered four children, and in 1909 sold almost all of the Compson property so that his oldest son, Quentin, III, might attend Harvard for one year and so that his daughter, Candace, might have a fine April wedding. *The Sound and the Fury, Absalom, Absalom!,* "That Evening Sun."

Compson, Jason Lycurgus, IV (1894–   ), son of Jason Lycurgus Compson, III and Carolyn Bascomb Compson. A childless bachelor and "more a Bascomb than a Compson," Jason sent himself to a Memphis school where he learned the cotton business. In 1928 he was robbed by his niece, Quentin, of nearly $7,000 about half of which was legally hers, left for her use by her mother. In 1933, upon the death of his mother, he committed Benjy, his brother, to the state asylum and sold the Old Compson Place to "a countryman who operated it as a boarding-house" (according to *The Sound and the Fury*); in 1943, (according to *The Mansion*) Flem Snopes bought the property, a transaction which Jason regretted, and his efforts to find a flaw in the title proved fruitless, "for Flem Snopes wasn't going to buy a title from anybody capable of having a flaw in it." *The Sound and the Fury, The Town, The Mansion,* "A Justice," "That Evening Sun."

Compson, Quentin (1891–June, 1910), the Jefferson-born son of

Jason Lycurgus Compson, III, and Carolyn Bascomb Compson. Taught by his father that "all men are just accumulations, dolls stuffed with sawdust swept up from the trash heaps," he "loved not his sister's body" nor "the idea of the incest which he would not commit, but some presbyterian concept of its eternal punishment." After spending a year at Harvard, financed by the sale of the last of the Compson property, he committed suicide in Cambridge, two months after his sister's wedding. *The Sound and the Fury, Absalom, Absalom!, The Mansion,* "That Evening Sun," "Lion," "A Justice."

Compson, Quentin (1911–   ), illegitimate daughter of Candace Compson. In 1928 she climbed down a drain pipe and ran off with a sideshow worker after taking nearly $7,000, part of which was rightfully hers, from her uncle Jason Compson. *The Sound and the Fury, The Mansion.*

Compson, Quentin MacLachan (1699–1783), son of a Glasgow printer. Orphaned, he was reared by his mother's family in the Perth highlands, from which he fled to Carolina and then to Kentucky with his grandson, Jason. *The Sound and the Fury.*

Compson, Governor Quentin MacLachan, son of Jason Lycurgus Compson and father of General Jason Lycurgus Compson, II. "The old governor was the last Compson who would not fail at everything he touched save longevity or suicide." *The Sound and the Fury.*

Comyn, an Irishman who served in the Royal Flying Corps during World War I. "Ad Astra."

Confrey, Max, owner and operator, with his wife Mame, of a restaurant in Jefferson. Amused by and cynical of the relationship between Joe Christmas and their waitress-call girl, Bobbie Allen, they referred to the naïve Joe as "Romeo" and to Bobbie as "the youth's companion." After the McEachern murder, they assisted in the beating and robbing of Joe. *Light in August.*

Conner (Connors), Buck, a Jefferson marshal and chief of police who helped rid the community of Montgomery Ward Snopes. *Sartoris, Light in August, The Town,* "Centaur in Brass," "The Waifs."

Convict (Plump), a Mississippian serving out a 199-year sentence for some unspecified crime. *The Wild Palms.*

Convict (Tall), a nameless hero during a Mississippi River flood.

This twenty-five-year-old delta innocent was serving a fifteen-year sentence for attempted train robbery, when "the old man" went on a rampage. For his sturdy and unbending effort to follow orders to rescue a pregnant woman caught in the flood, he was rewarded with an additional ten years on his sentence "for attempted escape." *The Wild Palms.*

Cooper, Minnie, a fading old maid who lived "with her invalid mother and a thin, sallow, unflagging aunt." She was "losing ground" but gained notoriety by her hysterical accusations of rape against harmless Will Mayes. "Dry September."

Corporal (Boggan, Brzewski, Stefan), the bastard son of a great French marshal. He was reared by two half-sisters, Marthe and Marya. He refused two "virtuous and solvent" candidates for a wife to take his revenge on his father with a Marseille whore, a "good girl," proving what love can do: "save a woman as well as damn her." He was leader of the "sit-down for peace" mutiny during action in France in 1918. Condemned to die by the marshal, he gladly took "that one last bitterest pill of martyrdom . . . the act of voluntarily relinquishing the privilege of ever knowing you were right." His death, at age thirty-three, was "the ace of trumps" as he and two thieves, Lapin and Horse, were shot while tied to rotten posts. His body, buried briefly in a cave near St. Mihiel, was apparently blown free by a bomb, was later recovered, and ultimately rested in the Tomb of the Unknown Soldier. *A Fable.*

Corrie, Miss. *See* Hogganbeck, Everbe Corinthia.

Cotton, Ernest, a Frenchman's Bend bachelor. He murdered Jack Houston because Houston won a law suit against Cotton concerning some shoats. Cotton is an early version of Mink Snopes. "The Hound."

Cowrie, Captain, an RAF officer. He shared Bridesman's hut at the aerodrome. *A Fable.*

Crain, Amos, a young married farmer in the Valley of Virginia. He was a neighbor of Roger Howes. "Artist at Home."

Cranston, Lily, a spinster who ran a summer resort in Cranston's Wells, Mississippi. "Doctor Martino."

Craw-Ford (Crawfish-ford), foster father of Sam Fathers. "A Justice."

Crawford, Dr., a sawmill doctor at Hoke's, a small railway station.

He treated Lion, Boon Hogganbeck, and Sam Fathers, in that order, after Old Ben was killed. "The Bear."

Crenshaw, Jack, a Revenue Department field agent. He did the "still hunting" in Yoknapatawpha County. *The Town.*

Crump, Lucas, a mail rider. *Idyll in the Desert.*

Cunninghame, an English sergeant during World War I. He tried to help Alec Gray. "Victory."

D

Damuddy. *See* Compson, "Damuddy."

Dan, a lotman employed by Roth Edmonds on his plantation near Jefferson. "The Fire and the Hearth."

Darl. *See* Bundren, Darl.

David, a seventeen-year-old wanderer who appeared in New Orleans. Penniless, jobless, and hungry, he "could have come from anywhere." He was "at peace with the world." "Out of Nazareth."

Davy, a young American who served in World War I and lost his leg. "The Leg."

Deacon, a Negro acquaintance of Quentin Compson in Cambridge. He marched in all the Cambridge parades and was one of the few people trusted by Quentin. *The Sound and the Fury.*

Delphine, the fourth wife of Ned William McCaslin. She was the Priest's cook in Jefferson. *The Reivers.*

De Montigny, Paul, a young man who was part Negro. Educated at the University of Virginia and Harvard, he was Elly's lover. He was killed when she deliberately crashed the car in which they were riding. "Elly."

De Spain, Major Cassius, father of Manfred de Spain, husband of Lula, and a major in the Confederate Army. He owned a hunting camp about twenty miles from Jefferson. He later sold the land to a lumber company. A feud with Ab Snopes resulted in the burning of de Spain's barn. He was sheriff of Yoknapatawpha County when Wash Jones killed his granddaughter, great-granddaughter, and Thomas Sutpen. *Absalom, Absalom!, The*

Hamlet, "Barn Burning," "The Bear," "Lion," "The Old People," "Delta Autumn."

De Spain, Major Hoxey, mayor of Jefferson. A graduate of Yale, he was "the town's lone rich middle-aged bachelor." "Centaur in Brass.

De Spain, Lula, the wife of Major Cassius de Spain. Her rug was damaged by Ab Snopes. "Barn Burning."

De Spain, Major Manfred, the son of Major Cassius de Spain. "Born into respectability," he graduated from West Point, served as a second lieutenant in Cuba, and returned to Jefferson "with a long jagged scar down one cheek." A banker and politician, mayor of Jefferson in 1904, he had frequent conflicts with Gavin Stevens, lusted after Eula Varner Snopes, succeeded in acquiring her as his mistress, and left for the west after Eula's suicide, giving "evident intention of not aiming to return to Jefferson." His twenty-three-year-old son was killed in World War II. *The Town, The Mansion,* "A Bear Hunt," "Shall Not Perish."

De Vitry, Chevalier Soeur-Blonde, a Parisian expatriate, mentor and influential friend of Ikkemotubbe. He originated the title "Doom" from *du homme.* "A Courtship," "Red Leaves," "The Old People."

Devries, Colonel, a graduate in 1941 of the University of Mississippi. Commissioned as a second lieutenant, this Jeffersonian led Negro troops overseas during World War II, returning with the rank of colonel and the Congressional Medal of Honor. He was a successful candidate for Congress, opposing C. Egglestone Snopes, and a pre-nomination campaign meeting of his provided one of the most humorous episodes in the Snopes saga. *The Mansion,* "By the People."

Dewey Dell. *See* Bundren, Dewey Dell.

Dick, Colonel Nathaniel G., the Ohio cavalry officer who halted the search for young Bayard Sartoris and Ringo. He later ordered the return of the Sartoris Negroes, mules, and chest of silver. *The Unvanquished.*

Dilazuck, owner of a Jefferson livery stable. *The Mansion.*

Dilsey, the Compson family cook. This wise Negress who "endured" was the mate of Roskus, mother of Frony, Versh, and

T.P., and grandmother of Luster. Her face wore "an expression at once fatalistic and of a child's astonished disappointment." As the Compson family disintegrated, Dilsey stood firm and reliable; in her old age she could say, "I seed de beginnin, en now I sees de endin." *The Sound and the Fury*, "That Evening Sun."

Doc, an Oxford "town boy" who made fun of Gowan Stevens' drinking manners. *Sanctuary*.

Doctor, a forty-eight-year-old nameless physician and the son of a doctor. He tried unsuccessfully to remain aloof from the odd behavior of his summer tenants, the Wilbournes. Married for twenty-three years with no children and little interest in living, he was forced from his detachment by the Wilbournes' strangely passionate relationship. *The Wild Palms*.

Dodge, Granby, an itinerant Mississippi preacher and some-time horse and mule trader. He was responsible for the murders of Old Anselm Holland and Probate Judge Dukinfield. "Smoke."

Don, a twenty-three-year-old American tourist in Italy. "Mistral."

Doom. *See* Ikkemotubbe.

Dough, James, a World War I veteran. Two years a corporal pilot in a French chassé escadrille, he lost his leg in combat. *Soldiers' Pay*.

Drake, Judge, a jurist from Jackson, Mississippi, father of Temple Drake Stevens and four sons. *Sanctuary*.

Drake, Temple. *See* Stevens, Temple Drake.

Drusilla. *See* Sartoris, Drusilla Hawk.

Du Pre, Virginia Sartoris (1839–1929), sister of Colonel John Sartoris. Widowed at the beginning of the Civil War at age twenty-three, she arrived (in 1869, according to *Sartoris* and "There Was a Queen"; in 1867, according to *The Unvanquished*) from Carolina to live with the colonel. "Spare and erect and brusque and uncompromising and kind," she told stories to the wrong people at the wrong time, and was extremely popular with young people. A reluctant passenger in young Bayard Sartoris' car, she failed to curb his passion for speed. She outlived all of the Sartorises except her great-great-great nephew, Benbow. She questioned the choice of the child's name, doubting that "because his name is Benbow he'll be any less a Sartoris and a scoundrel and a fool." *Sartoris, Sanctuary*,

The Unvanquished, Requiem for a Nun, "All the Dead Pilots," "There Was a Queen."

Dukinfield, Judge, a Jefferson probate judge. A widower of more than sixty years, he was murdered by a gunman hired by Granby Dodge. His mysterious death provided occasion for a piece of brilliant detective work by County Attorney Gavin Stevens. *The Town, The Mansion,* "Smoke."

Durley, a Frenchman's Bend resident. "Spotted Horses."

E

Edmonds, Alice, wife of McCaslin Edmonds, mother of Zachary Edmonds. She taught Tennie Beauchamp's daughter, Fonsiba, "to read and write too a little." "The Bear."

Edmonds, Carothers (Roth) (March, 1898—   ), the unmarried son of Zachary Edmonds. He was father of a boy by Tennie's Jim Beauchamp's granddaughter, but refused to marry his son's mother, leaving money for her with Uncle Isaac McCaslin. His life was harassed by the complications that his distant Negro relative and near neighbor, Lucas Beauchamp, introduced. *Intruder in the Dust, The Town,* "Go Down, Moses," "Delta Autumn," "Race at Morning," "Gold Is Not Always," "A Point of Law," "The Fire and the Hearth."

Edmonds, McCaslin (Cass) (1850—   ), the great-grandson of Lucius Quintus Carothers McCaslin, husband of Alice, and father of Zachary Edmonds. He helped serve as his cousin Isaac McCaslin's mentor of woodsmanship and inherited the land which his cousin refused to own. For Lucas Beauchamp he built a house and allotted him a specific acreage to be farmed as he saw fit. *The Reivers,* "Was," "The Fire and the Hearth," "The Bear," "Delta Autumn," "The Old People."

Edmonds, Zachary (Zack), the son of McCaslin and Alice Edmonds. He lost his wife when his son, Carothers Edmonds, was born in 1898. He took in Molly Beauchamp as a nurse for the baby and was nearly murdered when Lucas Beauchamp demanded Molly, his wife, back. *The Reivers,* "The Fire and the Hearth."

Ek, a hill-country man. A champion yarn-spinner, he was shot in the shoulder for telling a tale that was true. "The Liar."

Elly (Ailanthia), an eighteen-year-old Jefferson resident of questionable reputation. She became Paul de Montigny's lover and then, because he would not marry her, she killed him and her own grandmother by deliberately wrecking the car in which they were riding. "Elly."

Emmy, the daughter of a dipsomaniac house painter. She was sixteen when Donald Mahon made love to her. When her father threatened to beat her to death, she left home, got a job sewing for a dressmaker, and later became the Reverend Joe Mahon's housekeeper. Her love for Donald never failed, even though when he returned from war, "the Donald she had known was dead" and the grievously wounded and scarred veteran was "a sorry substitute." *Soldiers' Pay.*

Ephraim, father of Paralee Sander, grandfather of Aleck Sander. *Intruder in the Dust, The Town.*

Ephum, the hired man at Ballenbaugh's camp and store. *The Reivers.*

Ernest, a Frenchman's Bend resident and one of the participants in the famous horse auction. "Spotted Horses."

Ernest, Mr., a hunter and farmer near Van Dorn. He was hard of hearing. "Race at Morning."

Eulalia. *See* Sutpen, Eulalia.

Eunice. *See* Roskus, Eunice.

Eunice, a cook for Horace Benbow. *Sartoris.*

Everbe Corinthia. *See* Hogganbeck, Everbe Corinthia.

Ewell, Bryan, a deputy in Jefferson. "An Error in Chemistry."

Ewell, Walter, a regular member of the de Spain hunting parties. He was one "whose rifle never missed." *The Mansion,* "The Bear," "The Old People," "Delta Autumn," "Race at Morning."

Ewing, Ira, a middle-aged Nebraska-born resident of Beverly Hills, California. "Golden Land."

Ewing, Mitch, a depot freight agent in Jefferson. "Hair."

Ewing, Samantha, the mother of Ira Ewing. She found the ease and moral laxity of California life unpalatable, and she wished only to return to Nebraska. "Golden Land."

Ewing, Voyd, the son of Ira Ewing. He was an effeminate young man who took great pains never to be alone in the presence of his father. "Golden Land."

F

Fairchild, Dawson, a novelist who looked like a "deceptively sedate walrus of middle age." He enjoyed watching all human beings, and if possible, making fools of some of them. He was "reasonably keen about people—sooner or later." *Mosquitoes.*

Falls, Will (Old Man Falls), a ninety-four-year-old poorhouse resident and friend of old Bayard Sartoris, he removed the wen from Bayard's face. *Sartoris.*

Farr, Cecily Saunders, the daughter of Robert and Minnie Saunders. "She was like a flower stalk or a young tree . . . her clear delicate being was nourished by sunlight and honey until even digestion was a beautiful function." Spoiled and conscious of her sexual attraction, she was unable to "submit" to marriage to fiancé Donald Mahon because of his scarred face, and gave herself to George Farr. *Soldiers' Pay.*

Farr, George, a love-tormented swain of Charlestown, Georgia. Considering himself "quite a man," he wooed, seduced, and wed Cecily Saunders. *Soldiers' Pay.*

Fathers, Sam (Had-Two Fathers), the son of a Chickasaw (Choctaw, according to "A Justice") chief, Ikkemotubbe, and a quadroon slave woman. He and his mother were sold to old Carothers McCaslin (according to "A Justice" they were sold to General Compson). A carpenter and woodsman, he tutored Isaac McCaslin in hunting, died shortly after the death of Old Ben, was buried beside Lion, the dog, and like them, was "taintless and incorruptible." "The Bear," "The Old People," "Delta Autumn," "A Justice," "Red Leaves."

Faulkner, Mr. (Mr. Bill), a hill-country farmer to whom Faulkner gave his own name. "Afternoon of a Cow."

Faulkner, Mrs., "Mr. Bill's" wife. "Afternoon of a Cow."

Faulkner, James, "Mr. Faulkner's" brother's son. "Afternoon of a Cow."

Faulkner, Malcolm, "Mr. Faulkner's" son. "Afternoon of a Cow."

Feinman, Colonel H. I., a New Valois airfield owner more interested in profit than in safety. *Pylon.*

Fentry, Stonewall Jackson, a poor farmer, resident of the very other end of the county, about thirty miles from Frenchman's Bend. He married a Thorpe girl just before she died and just before she bore an illegitimate child, Buck Thorpe. Fentry was the only man on a jury who voted not to acquit Odum Bookwright for the murder of Thorpe. "Tomorrow."

Ffollansbye, a member of the Royal Air Force in World War I. "Thrift," "All the Dead Pilots."

Flint, a young intern who introduced Harry Wilbourne to Charlotte Rittenmeyer in New Orleans. *The Wild Palms.*

Flint, Ellie Pritchel, the daughter of Wesley Pritchel. This "dimwitted spinster" met and married Joel Flint when she was almost forty. Flint murdered Ellie and her father. "An Error in Chemistry."

Flint, Joel (Signor Canova), one-time pitchman in a traveling street carnival. He murdered his wife, Ellie, and his father-in-law, Wesley Pritchel. His disappearing act was foiled by Gavin Stevens. "An Error in Chemistry."

Fortinbride, Brother, a Methodist lay preacher. He served as a private in Colonel John Sartoris' regiment and informally officiated at Rosa Millard's funeral. *The Unvanquished,* "Vendée," "The Unvanquished."

Fox, Matt, a Jefferson barber. "Hair."

Fraser, a Yoknapatawpha distiller who took care of Monk Odlethrop when Monk was a boy. "Monk."

Fraser, a member of Major Manfred de Spain's hunting parties. "A Bear Hunt."

Fraser, Doyle, the owner of a store in the Beat Four area near which Vinson Gowrie was murdered. *Intruder in the Dust.*

Frazier, Judge, a Yoknapatawpha County jurist. He tried the Buck Thorpe murder case. "Tomorrow."

Freeman, a Frenchman's Bend farmer. He was one of the purchasers of Flem Snopes's infamous spotted horses. *The Hamlet.*

Frony, the daughter of Dilsey. She married a pullman porter and lived in St. Louis. Later she moved to Memphis, "since Dilsey refused to go further than that," to make a home for her mother. *The Sound and the Fury,* "That Evening Sun."

Frost, Mark, a pale young man and singularly inert companion of

Dorothy Jameson. He considered himself "the best poet in New Orleans." *Mosquitoes.*

G

Gabe, the Jefferson blacksmith. *The Reivers.*

Gambrell, C. L., a Mississippi state penitentiary warden. He was murdered by Monk Odlethrop. "Monk."

Gant, Eunice, a sales clerk at Wildermark's store in Jefferson. *The Town.*

Gant, Jim, a stock trader and father of Zilphia Gant. When his daughter was two years old, he ran away with Mrs. Vinson to Memphis, where he was murdered by his wife. *Miss Zilphia Gant.*

Gant, Mrs. Jim, the wife of Jim Gant, mother of Zilphia. After she was deserted by her husband, she went to Memphis and killed Gant and his lover. Mrs. Gant then moved to Jefferson with her two-year-old daughter, Zilphia, and started a dressmaking shop. She made her frustrated daughter as neurotic as she herself was and died after she had chased away Zilphia's legal husband. *Miss Zilphia Gant.*

Gant, Zilphia, the daughter of Jim Gant. Born near Frenchman's Bend and reared in Jefferson, she learned to hate and distrust men from her paranoid mother and from her own unconsummated marriage. She adopted the daughter (Zilphia) of her painter-husband after his death, and taught the girl the same lessons of bitterness which she had been taught. By profession she was a dressmaker. *Miss Zilphia Gant.*

Garraway, an old man "with an old man's dim, cloudy eyes." He ran a small dingy store at Seminary Hill, outside Jefferson, and because of his inflexible Puritan beliefs was the first to move his account from Colonel Bayard Sartoris' bank when Manfred de Spain became its president. *The Town.*

Gary, Dr., a Charlestown, Georgia physician. He served in a French hospital during World War I. Small, dapper and bald, he was "much in demand, both professionally and socially" in Charlestown. *Soldiers' Pay.*

Gatewood, Jabbo, the son of Uncle Noon Gatewood. He was the best mechanic in the county. *The Town.*

Gatewood, Uncle Noon, a powerful blacksmith whose shop was near the edge of Jefferson. *The Town.*

Gawtrey, Steve, a houseguest of Harrison Blair. "Fox Hunt."

Generalissimo. *See* Marshal.

George, a seven-year-old opportunist. He lived with his parents in Jefferson and ran errands for his uncle Rodney. The family cook once said to him, "If you ain't rich time you twenty-one, hit will be because the law done abolished money or done abolished you." "That Will Be Fine."

George, a student at Oxford and friend of Davy. He was commissioned by Davy to find the amputated leg to make sure it was dead. "The Leg."

George, a cook for a Greek ship. His affection for his shipmate, Carl, was shaken, but not broken, by the other's infidelity in Naples. "Divorce in Naples."

Gibson, Dilsey. *See* Dilsey.

Gibson, Will, a country store proprietor, probably an early version of Will Varner. "The Liar."

Gihon, an FBI agent who came to Jefferson to check on communist-card carrying Linda Snopes Kohl, offering her "immunity for names." *The Mansion.*

Gihon, Danny, the only son of Mrs. Margaret Noonan Gihon. He graduated from petty theft to an apparently successful career in crime in Chicago. "Pennsylvania Station."

Gihon, Mrs. Margaret Noonan, a New York widow, mother of Danny. Her rewards for motherhood included the robbery of her coffin money by her own son. "Pennsylvania Station."

Gillespie, a Frenchman's Bend farmer, father of Mack. The Bundrens stopped overnight at his place on the way to Jefferson and Darl Bundren set fire to his barn. *As I Lay Dying.*

Gilligan, Joe, an Army private. This outwardly hard-boiled soldier adopted dying Donald Mahon as his charge, with the help of Margaret Powers. A perceptive, sensitive man, this "nice fool" gave more than he received and refused to acknowledge that he would never do anything "without considering someone else's feelings." *Soldiers' Pay.*

Gilman, one of the twin sons of a New England justice of the peace. He and his family ingeniously tricked a group of professional bootleggers. "Country Mice."

Ginotta, Joe, a New Orleans restaurant operator and bootlegger. He was the brother of Pete. *Mosquitoes.*

Ginotta, Pete, the chain-smoking boyfriend of Jenny Steinbauer. He accompanied her on the Maurier yachting party. His family operated a restaurant-bootlegging business in New Orleans. *Mosquitoes.*

Ginsfarb, a Jewish airplane acrobat. His penuriousness caused him to take chances in his "death drag" jump, resulting in a broken leg. "Death Drag."

Girl, The, a "Marseille whore" who was "leading through her own fate, necessity, compulsions, a life which was not her life." She was supposedly married to the Corporal and traveled with his two half-sisters, Marthe and Marya, to try to prevent his death. After he died she returned to Marseille, resuming her profession to support an aged grandmother. *A Fable.*

Gombault, a United States marshal, "a lean, clean old man who chewed tobacco, who had been born and lived in the country all his life." *Requiem for a Nun, The Town,* "The Tall Men."

Goodwin, Mrs. *See* Lamar, Ruby.

Goodwin, Lee, a Yoknapatawpha County bootlegger. He saw service as a cavalry sergeant in the Philippines, during which he killed a soldier "over one of those nigger women." He was released from Leavenworth to enlist during World War I and earned two medals for action in France. He was sent back to Leavenworth, released on Congressional appeal, and returned to the county with his faithful mistress, Ruby Lamar. Their ensuing bootlegging activities were abruptly shattered by the arrival of Temple Drake and her drunken companion, Gowan Stevens. Goodwin was unjustly charged with the murder of Tommy, who had been trying to protect Temple; he was tried, defended unsuccessfully by Horace Benbow, and lynched by an angry mob inflamed by Temple's perjurious testimony. *Sanctuary.*

Goodyhay, J. C., an ex-Marine sergeant who "got religion" during the war. This self-styled preacher provided work and lodging in north Mississippi for Mink Snopes on Mink's journey from prison back to Jefferson in 1946. *The Mansion.*

Gordon, a thirty-six-year-old sculptor. Proud, lonely, and arrogant, he may have been a genius in his field of art, but he found it difficult to communicate with other human beings. His feminine ideal was "a virgin with no legs to leave me, no arms to hold me, no head to talk to me." *Mosquitoes.*

Gowan, Judge, the Jefferson judge before whom Lucas Beauchamp and George Wilkins were brought for making whiskey. He ordered the stills destroyed and dismissed the case. "The Fire and the Hearth," "A Point of Law."

Gower, the stout district attorney who prosecuted Harry Wilbourne. *The Wild Palms.*

Gowrie, Bilbo, a son of Nub Gowrie of Beat Four, and twin of Vardaman. *Intruder in the Dust.*

Gowrie, Bryan, the third son of Nub Gowrie. He was the "cohering element," the one who actually ran the family farm which supported the clan. *Intruder in the Dust.*

Gowrie, Crawford, the second of Nub Gowrie's six sons. Drafted on November 2, 1918, he deserted on November 10; for this he spent a year in Leavenworth. After his release, he ran liquor from New Orleans to Memphis, and later settled down in Beat Four in the lumber business. He murdered his brother-partner, Vinson, when Vinson discovered that Crawford was trying to cheat him. *Intruder in the Dust.*

Gowrie, Forrest, the oldest son of Nub Gowrie. For twenty years he was manager of a delta cotton plantation near Vicksburg. *Intruder in the Dust.*

Gowrie, Nub, a one-armed Frenchman's Bend bootlegger. "A violent foul-mouthed godless old man," he learned with grief that one of his six sons, Crawford, had murdered the youngest, Vinson. *Intruder in the Dust, The Town, The Mansion.*

Gowrie, Vardaman, one of the six sons of Nub Gowrie, and twin of Bilbo. The twins spent their nights hunting foxes and their days sleeping on the front gallery. *Intruder in the Dust.*

Gowrie, Vinson, the youngest son of Beat Four bootlegger, Nub Gowrie. Murdered at age twenty-eight, he was "the first Gowrie who could sign his name to a check and have any bank honor it." *Intruder in the Dust.*

Gragnon, Charles (1871–1918), a major-general and division commander of French forces during World War I. He was "intended by fate itself to be the perfect soldier." Reared in a

Pyrenean orphanage, at seventeen he enlisted as a private; by 1914 he had a "splendid record" as a desert colonel of Spahis. Somewhere he lost "the old habit" of "almost monotonous success" when the men in his division refused to fight. "Too tough to be scared and too hard to be hurt," he refused an "honorable" death, insisting that he be shot in the back to "make the whole world see that not the enemy but his own men did it." *A Fable.*

Graham, Eustace, the district attorney of Jefferson during the trial of Lee Goodwin for the murder of Tommy. He had a club foot "which had elected him to the office he now held." He worked his way through the state university, and two years after graduation from law school he was elected to the state legislature. *Sartoris, Sanctuary.*

Gratton, Eustace, a man who served on the British front during World War I. *Sartoris.*

Gray, Alexander, a Scots-born captain in the British army, awarded the military cross and distinguished service medal, twice wounded and twice hospitalized. He spent his last years selling matches in London. "Victory."

Gray, Johnny, a young New Orleans thug. He protected a girl from the Wop, at the expense of his own life. "The Kid Learns."

Gray, Matthew, a Scots ship builder, father of Alexander Gray. He resented his son's enlistment and attempts to become a gentleman. "Victory."

Green, Captain, a Georgian who raised a company during World War I and got his commission from the governor. "He might have been a good officer, he might have been anything," but he was killed in action. *Soldiers' Pay.*

Grenier, Louis (–1837), a Huguenot younger son, one of the first three settlers of Yoknapatawpha County. "A Paris educated architect," he brought the first slaves into the county, became the first cotton planter, had an imported English carriage and "what was said to be the finest matched team outside of Natchez or Nashville." A hundred years after his arrival nothing was left but the name of his plantation "and his own fading corrupted legend. . . ." *Intruder in the Dust, Requiem for a Nun, The Town, The Reivers.*

Grier, Peter (1923–42), the older son of Res Grier. At age nineteen he enlisted in the U.S. Army and was later killed in action. "Two Soldiers," "Shall Not Perish."

Grier, Res, a Frenchman's Bend farmer and the father of two sons. He accidentally set Reverend Whitfield's church on fire while he was taking off the shingles. "Shall Not Perish," "Shingles for the Lord," "Two Soldiers."

Grierson, Miss Emily, a Jefferson spinster, "a tradition, a duty, and a care." When she was about thirty, her father died and she was left alone. Courted and jilted by Homer Barron, she poisoned him, but kept his corpse "to cling to that which had robbed her." "A Rose for Emily."

Grimm, Eustace, the son of Ab Snopes's youngest sister. He worked for Flem Snopes in the Frenchman's Bend store and helped pull off the Old Frenchman's Place swindle. *As I Lay Dying, The Hamlet,* "Lizards in Jamshyd's Courtyard."

Grimm, Percy, a twenty-five-year-old captain in the Mississippi National Guard. He could "never forgive his parents" for delaying his birth so that he was too young to serve in World War I. Fanatical in his devotion to wearing a uniform, "with fierce and constrained joy," he almost single-handedly hunted down the tormented Joe Christmas and castrated him in a bloody slaughter in the Reverend Gail Hightower's kitchen. *Light in August.*

Grinnup, Dan, a "dirty man with a tobacco-stained beard," a survivor of one of the original settlers of the county, Louis Grenier. He acted unofficially as hack driver for the Priest livery stable in Jefferson. *The Reivers.*

Grinnup, Lonnie, a descendant of Louis Grenier; guardian of a deaf and dumb boy named Joe. "A cheerful middle-aged man with the mind and face of a child," he was murdered by Boyd Ballenbaugh. *Intruder in the Dust,* "Hand Upon the Waters."

Grove, Lena, born and reared near Doane's Mill, Alabama. She was left an orphan at twelve. Ignorant, innocent, and fertile, she became pregnant when about twenty. After realizing that she had been deserted by the unborn child's father, Lucas Burch, she left home with thirty-five cents in her pocket to search for him, encountering in the course of her travels kindness and evil, and the comforting adoration of Byron Bunch.

Not much more than half his age, she had "already outlived him twice over." *Light in August.*

Grover Cleveland. *See* Winbush, Grover.

Grumby, Major, the almost coldly inhuman leader of Grumby's Independents, a troop of fifty to sixty men who terrified the countryside after the departure of the Yankees, raiding and burning, under a signed commission by General Forrest. He was killed by Bayard Sartoris in revenge for Grumby's murder of Granny Rosa Millard. *The Unvanquished, The Hamlet,* "Vendée."

Grummet, the owner of a hardware store in Mottstown where the Bundrens bought ten cents worth of cement for Cash Bundren's broken leg. *As I Lay Dying.*

Gualdres, Captain Sebastian, a middle-aged Argentine army officer. He married Mrs. Melisandre Backus Harriss Stevens' daughter and enlisted in the U.S. Army near the beginning of World War II. "Knight's Gambit."

Gus, a professional bootlegger. He and his brother-partner were thoroughly "taken" by a New England justice of the peace and his twin sons. "Country Mice."

Gus. *See* Robyn, Patricia.

Guster, a Negro servant for the Mallison family. *The Town.*

H

Habersham, Mrs., a welfare aide in Jefferson. She helped the younger Grier boy get to Memphis to join his brother. "Two Soldiers."

Habersham, Eunice (Emily), a descendant of an old Jefferson family. Most of her days were spent quietly and frugally in her home at the edge of town, except when she was called upon to act in situations too explosive for most people. Two such occasions concerned the return of Byron Snopes's four half-breed children and the gathering of evidence to prove the innocence of accused murderer Lucas Beauchamp. *Intruder in the Dust, The Town.*

Habersham, Mrs. Martha, a neighbor and friend of the Sartoris family. She was instrumental in effecting the marriage between Drusilla Hawk and Colonel John Sartoris; she also contributed three bottles of Madeira for the wedding reception. *The Unvanquished,* "Skirmish at Sartoris."

Habersham, Samuel, a physician, one of the first three settlers in Jefferson. With his motherless eight-year-old son, he arrived from Tennessee as the government Indian agent. For some time the pioneer settlement was called Habersham. *Requiem for a Nun, The Town.*

Had-Two-Fathers. *See* Fathers, Sam.

Hagood, the editor of the New Orleans newspaper for which the reporter-narrator worked. He was patient and generous to an almost unbelievable degree. *Pylon.*

Hait, Lonzo, a Jefferson horse and mule trader. Husband of Mannie Hait, he had a business partnership with I. O. Snopes. The business consisted of tying mules to the railroad tracks and collecting insurance not just for the mules but for the rope as well. His career ended when he himself was run over by a train, enabling his wife to collect $8,500. *The Town, The Mansion,* "Mule in the Yard."

Hait, Mannie, the childless widow of Lonzo Hait. She "sold her husband to the railroad company for eight thousand per cent profit," and got the better of I. O. Snopes on two business transactions. *The Town,* "Mule in the Yard."

Halliday, the Mottstown citizen who first recognized and grabbed Joe Christmas casually walking back and forth in broad daylight, after the murder of Joanna Burden. *Light in August.*

Hamp, a Negro servant of Miss Worsham and the brother of Aunt Molly Beauchamp. "Go Down, Moses."

Hampton, Hope, the sheriff of Yoknapatawpha County after World War II. A "gigantic man" in his fifties, he had "sense and character enough to run the county and then fill the rest of the jobs with cousins and inlaws who had failed to make a living at everything else they ever tried." Prodded and aided by two boys and an old maid, he successfully solved the Gowrie murder case and protected Lucas Beauchamp from being lynched. *Intruder in the Dust.*

Hampton, Hub (Hubert), a county sheriff who helped de-

Snopesize Jefferson. He had "little hard pale eyes that never seemed to need to blink at all." He died in office and was succeeded by his son. *The Hamlet, The Town, The Mansion, The Reivers,* "The Waifs."

Hampton, Hubert, Jr., the son of Sheriff Hampton. He inherited his father's job and his "capacity to stay on the best of political terms with his alternating opposite number." *The Mansion.*

Handy, Professor, a Memphis band leader. His group played for the Jefferson Christmas cotillion. *The Town.*

Harker, the night engineer at the Jefferson power plant. *The Town,* "Centaur in Brass."

Harker, Otis, a relative of the night engineer. He succeeded Grover Cleveland Winbush as Jefferson night marshal. *The Town.*

Harris, a French Quarter resident. He carried on an incessant feud with his neighbor Juan Venturia. "The Rosary."

Harris, a Jefferson resident. He rented his car to Ginsfarb for the flying act. "Death Drag."

Harris, a Grenier County farmer and victim of Ab Snopes's barn-burning. *The Hamlet,* "Barn Burning."

Harris, the proprietor of the Jefferson livery stable. He played poker with Eustace Graham. *Sanctuary.*

Harris, owner of a flying circus. "Honor."

Harris, Meloney, a maid for Belle Mitchell. After borrowing money belonging to the Baptist church from Simon Strother, she left Mitchell's to start a beauty parlor. *Sartoris.*

Harrison, Sergeant, a Union soldier. Bayard Sartoris and Ringo shot a horse he was riding from under him. *The Unvanquished,* "Ambuscade."

Harriss (Harris), a New Orleans gangster and "bootleg czar." He married gently educated, Jefferson-bred Melisandre Backus, and by her had a son and a daughter. After his father-in-law's death he transformed the "simple familiar red-ink north Mississippi cotton plantation" into a "Long Island horse farm." He died of an "occupational disease," murder by a competitor. *The Mansion,* "Knight's Gambit."

Harriss, Miss, the daughter of Melisandre Backus Harriss Stevens and sister of Max. She married Captain Sebastian Gualdres near the beginning of World War II. "Knight's Gambit."

Harriss, Max, the son of Melisandre Backus Harriss Stevens and a
New Orleans gangster. He enlisted in the U.S. Army on December 6, 1941. "Knight's Gambit."

Harriss, Melisandre Backus. *See* Stevens, Melisandre Backus Harriss.

Harry, Mr. (**Mistairy**). *See* Sentry.

Hatcher, Louis, a Negro. He impressed young Quentin Compson
with his tale of surviving the flood when it got as wet in Jefferson as it had in Johnstown, Penn. *The Sound and the Fury.*

Hawk, Dennison (1853–   ), the son of Dennison and Louisa
Hawk, brother of Drusilla Hawk Sartoris. He was married in
1875, and studied law in Montgomery, Alabama. *The Unvanquished,* "Raid."

Hawk, Drusilla. *See* Sartoris, Drusilla Hawk.

Hawk, Mrs. Louisa, the sister of Rosa Millard, wife of Dennison
Hawk, and mother of Dennison Hawk and Drusilla Hawk Sartoris. Widowed during the Civil War, her Reconstruction activities included effecting a marriage between her daughter and
Colonel John Sartoris. She and her family lived at Hawkhurst,
Gihon County, Alabama. *The Unvanquished.*

Hawkshaw. *See* Stribling, Henry.

Head, Sydney Herbert, a graduate of Harvard and hard-headed
businessman of South Bend, Indiana. On April 25, 1910, he did
what he later regretted bitterly: married Candace Compson.
The Sound and the Fury.

Henry. *See* Beauchamp, Henry.

Henry, the Governor of Mississippi to whom Gavin Stevens and
Temple Drake Stevens appealed for clemency for Nancy Mannigoe. *Requiem for a Nun.*

Hightower, Gail, a one-time Presbyterian minister. Jefferson cynics argued that the "D. D." after his name stood for "done
damned." The son of an antislavery minister-father, grandson
of a hard-riding grandfather shot while galloping off after a
chicken raid, Gail was locked out of his church, and forced to
resign after the disgraceful behavior and suicide of his sluttish
wife, but he refused to leave Jefferson. The only friend of Byron
Bunch, he was forced to face real life and decisions with the
coming of Lena Grove and Joe Christmas to the town. *Light in
August.*

Hightower, Mrs. Gail, the only child of a Presbyterian minister, and wife of the Jefferson minister. During two years of courtship they exchanged notes in a hollow tree on the campus, and then one night "she spoke suddenly and savagely of marriage." They were married immediately following his graduation, after which he never once saw either desperation or passion on her face. After several prolonged weekends in Memphis she was sent to a sanitorium, returning apparently cured. Several months later she left for another weekend in Memphis, registered in a hotel under a fictitious name as the wife of another man, and was found dead, having jumped or fallen from the hotel window. *Light in August.*

Hines, Eupheus, a one-time railroad brakeman from Arkansas. This "incredibly dirty" religious fanatic arrived in Mottstown, near Jefferson, and preached white supremacy at revival meetings in Negro churches. His wild fanaticism resulted from the union of his daughter, Milly, to a supposedly "Mexican" circus hand, and the birth of their son, Joe Christmas. Suspecting that the circus hand was part Negro, Hines killed him, put the child in an orphanage, and spent the next thirty years acting as "God's chosen instrument" in reviling the Negro, "the pollution and abomination" of the earth. His greatest moment came when he urged Jeffersonians to lynch his grandson, "the devil's spawn." *Light in August.*

Hines, Mrs. Eupheus, the long-suffering, pathetic wife of Eupheus Hines and grandmother of Joe Christmas, whom she "had never seen as a man" until he was in jail on a charge of murder. A "dumpy, fat little woman," she waited five years before she dared ask her husband what he had done with their bastard grandchild, and over thirty years before she finally saw Joe Christmas, just before his bloody death. *Light in August.*

Hines, Milly, the daughter of Eupheus and Mrs. Hines. When the time came for her to deliver her child, sired by a so-called "Mexican" circus hand, this eighteen-year-old "abomination of womanflesh" had no medical assistance. Her father refused to go for a physician, believing that the devil should "gather his own crop; he was the one that laid it by." Milly died in childbirth, and the son grew up to be known as Joe Christmas, the "white nigger." *Light in August.*

Hipps, Buck, a Texan. With Flem Snopes he brought in and auctioned off in Frenchman's Bend a herd of wild Texas ponies. *The Hamlet,* "Spotted Horses."

Hogganbeck, Boon, inheritor of Chickasaw blood, "he had neither profession, job nor trade and owned one vice and one virtue: whiskey, and that absolute and unquestioning fidelity to Major de Spain" and to McCaslin Edmonds. Boon took over the care and training of Lion, but after shooting at Old Ben, the bear, five times and missing each time, he let Lion sleep with Sam Fathers, saying, "I ain't fit to sleep with him." However, it was Boon who, aided by Lion, ultimately conquered Old Ben. In 1905 he was assistant stable foreman for Maury Priest in Jefferson, and facts-of-life mentor for young Lucius Priest. Later he became the town marshal at Hoke's, a small railway station. Also in 1905 he married Everbe Corinthia and fathered a son, Lucius. "He had the mind of a child, the heart of a horse, and the little hard shoe-button eyes without depth or meanness or generosity or viciousness or gentleness or anything else." *The Town, The Reivers,* "The Old People," "The Bear," "Delta Autumn."

Hogganbeck, David, a steamboat pilot. He strenuously courted Herman Basket's sister, but did not win her. "A Courtship."

Hogganbeck, Everbe Corinthia, a one-time "employee" at Reba Rivers' house of prostitution in Memphis. Originally from Kiblett, Arkansas, she changed her name and her way of life upon arriving in Memphis, following Lucius Priest's vigorous and bloody defense of her virtue. In 1905 she married Boon Hogganbeck, and they had one son. *The Reivers.*

Hogganbeck, Lucius (Luke), the son of Boon and Everbe Corinthia Hogganbeck, named after young Lucius Priest. Married the father of three children, he owned a Model T Ford and ran a jitney passenger-hauling business. *The Town, The Mansion, The Reivers.*

Hogganbeck, Melissa, the world affairs teacher of Chick Mallison. She taught American history "in that anachronistic vacuum which was the Female Academy." *The Town,* "Knight's Gambit."

Holcomb, Ashley, a childhood friend of Chick Mallison. *The Town.*

Holcomb, Beth, a northern Mississippi housewife who provided food and work for Mink Snopes as he patiently trudged toward Memphis to buy a gun after his release from Parchman prison in 1946. *The Mansion.*

Holland, the jury foreman during the Buck Thorpe murder case. "Tomorrow."

Holland, Anselm (Old Man Anse), a farmer who lived near Frenchman's Bend. He married Cornelia Mardis and fathered twin sons, Anselm and Virginius. A "crazed, hate-ridden old man," he owned two thousand acres of some of the best land in the country, some of which at one time he rented to Ab Snopes and to V. K. Ratliff's father. He was murdered by his wife's distant relative, Granby Dodge. *The Hamlet,* "Smoke," "Fool About a Horse."

Holland, Anselm (Young Anse), the twin brother of Virginius and son of Anselm and Cornelia Mardis Holland. He ran away from home before he was twenty and stayed away ten years. At one time he was arrested and tried for making whiskey, and was sentenced to the penitentiary but pardoned after eight months for good behavior. He was "a dark, silent, aquiline-faced man whom both neighbors and strangers let severely alone." Young Anse received from his father's estate "two full sets of mule harness." "Smoke."

Holland, Cornelia Mardis, the wife of old Anselm Holland. She died while her twin sons were still children. "Smoke."

Holland, Virginius, the twin brother of Anselm, son of Anselm and Cornelia Mardis Holland. In his family Virginius acted as mediator, was "cursed for his pains by both father and brother." Before his father's death he lived with Granby Dodge, a remote kinsman. He inherited all of his father's property. "Smoke."

Holmes, Jack, a member of a strangely-related trio, including Roger and Laverne Shumann, which toured the country taking part in air shows. One fact about Holmes: he performed the delayed parachute jump; one unknown fact: whether he or Roger was the father of young Jack Shumann. *Pylon.*

Holston, Mrs., the manager of the Holston House during the Reconstruction period. *The Unvanquished,* "Skirmish at Sartoris."

Holston, Alexander (–1839), one of the first three settlers in Jefferson. A bachelor, he was "half groom and half bodyguard to Doctor Samuel Habersham, and half-nurse and half-tutor to the doctor's eight-year-old motherless son." He established the tavern known as the Holston House. *Requiem for a Nun, The Town.*

Hood, Parsham (Uncle Possum), a stately old Negro "with perfectly white moustaches and an imperial." He sheltered Lucius Priest and aided the Hogganbeck-Ned-Lucius Priest trio in their horse race. *The Reivers.*

Hooper, a traveling religious speaker, with a face like a thwarted Sunday-school superintendent. *Mosquitoes.*

Hope, L. Claude W., a Royal Navy midshipman who bravely served his country in torpedo missions during World War I. "Turnabout."

Horse (Casse-tête), a "squat simian-like man" with the "peaceful and patient fidelity of a blind dog." A murderer, with hands too strong, he shared a cell in France during World War I with Lapin and the Corporal. *A Fable.*

Houston, Jack (–1908), a resident of Frenchman's Bend, a "sulking and sulling" widower for years after his adored wife Lucy was killed by his prime stallion. This prosperous "high-nosed" farmer was shot and killed in 1908 by Mink Snopes as a result of a lawsuit concerning a yearling calf (according to *The Hamlet*); he was killed by Ernest Cotton as a result of a lawsuit concerning some shoats (according to "The Hound"). *As I Lay Dying, The Hamlet, The Town, The Mansion,* "The Hound."

Houston, Lucy Pate, the wife of Jack Houston. As a young girl she had tried to force Houston to pass the first grade. When she was twenty-four she married Houston and was killed in the same year by the stallion her husband had bought. *The Hamlet*

Hovis, a cashier at Manfred de Spain's bank. *The Town.*

Hovis, Mrs., a Jefferson do-gooder who helped try to cure Uncle Willy Christian. "Uncle Willy."

Howes, Anne, the wife of Roger Howes. She had a brief affair with the poet John Blair. "Artist at Home."

Howes, Darrel (Dorry House), an artist and stranger in town. *Idyll in the Desert.*

Howes, Roger, a middle-aged novelist, resident of the Valley o

Virginia. Married, the father of two children, he discovered that his house guest, John Blair, was not only enjoying his room and board, but also his wife. "Artist at Home."

Hughes, Manny, a post office clerk. *Idyll in the Desert.*

Hule, the younger son in a Tennessee family. He was shot and killed by his brother Vatch while trying to help Major Saucier Weddel escape. "Mountain Victory."

Hulett, the judge's clerk who tried to make Lucas Beauchamp behave with humility during the abortive divorce action taken by Molly Beauchamp. "The Fire and the Hearth."

I

diot, a helpless man with cornflower-blue eyes. He was vigorously protected by his bootlegger brother. He was a forerunner of Benjy Compson. "The Kingdom of God."

kkemotubbe (Doom, David Callicoat), the son of Issetibbeha's sister (according to "Red Leaves" Doom was Issetibbeha's father). A Chickasaw chief, he and his people owned the land before it passed to Sutpen and Major de Spain. In his youth he ran away to New Orleans, returning seven years later with a quadroon slave who was to be the mother of Sam Fathers and with a gold snuff-box filled with an influential white powder. His cousin, Moketubbe, who was to be the successor to Issetibbeha, abdicated immediately, and Ikkemotubbe became "The Man." Two years later he sold the quadroon, as well as the man to whom he had married her while she was pregnant, and her child to Carothers McCaslin. *The Sound and the Fury, Requiem for a Nun, The Town,* "The Old People," "The Bear," "A Justice," "Delta Autumn," "Red Leaves," "A Courtship."

ngrum, Willy, the Jefferson town marshal during the Lucas Beauchamp-Gowrie affair. *Intruder in the Dust.*

sham, an old Negro camp helper at the de Spain-McCaslin camp. "Delta Autumn."

som, the Negro driver for Horace Benbow. *Sanctuary.*

ssetibbeha, the son of Doom (according to "Red Leaves"), the

uncle of Doom (according to *The Town*, "Old People," "A
Courtship," "A Justice"). He was nineteen when he became
chief of the Chickasaws. He raised and sold Negroes, and
traveled to Europe on the profits. Decades later one of his
granddaughters married the twenty-five-year-old son of old Dr
Samuel Habersham. When he died he was buried with a dog, a
horse, and a slave. *Big Woods, Requiem for a Nun, The Town*
"The Old People," "Red Leaves," "Interlude," "A Courtship,"
"A Justice."

J

Jake, a Negro servant of Judge Allison. "Beyond."

Jake, the driver of the rented car in the death-drag act performed
by Ginsfarb and Jock. "Death Drag."

Jameson, Dorothy, an amateur painter. Men, sooner or later, "in
evitably ran out on her," except for Mark Frost, and "in his
case . . . it was sheer inertia more than anything else." Before
going to New Orleans to live she spent two years in Greenwich
Village and a year abroad. *Mosquitoes.*

Jarrod, Hubert, a native of Oklahoma. Educated at Yale, he be
longed to the right clubs and had plenty of money to spend
Nevertheless, he had to compete with old Dr. Martino for the
affection of his own fiancée, Louise King. "Doctor Martino."

Jean-Baptiste, a simple workman and lonely Frenchman who in
America yearned for his native land. "Home."

Jenny. *See* Steinbauer, Genevieve.

Jesus, a jealous husband and murderer of Nancy. "That Evening
Sun."

Jewel. *See* Bundren, Jewel.

Jiggs, an airplane mechanic for Roger Shumann. He abandoned
his wife and two children in Kansas. *Pylon.*

Jim, a Negro assistant to Pat Stamper. He "could take any piece
of horseflesh which still had life in it and retire to whatever
closed building or shed was empty and handy and then, with a
quality of actual legerdemain, reappear with something which
the beast's own dam would not recognize, let alone its recent
owner." *The Hamlet.*

Jingus, a Negro servant of the Hawk family. He showed young Bayard Sartoris his first railroad. *The Unvanquished,* "Raid."

Job, the old janitor of Judge Dukinfield. *The Town,* "Smoke."

Jobaker, a full-blooded Chickasaw, a market hunter, and fisherman who "consorted with nobody, black or white" except Sam Fathers. "The Old People."

Joby, the husband of Louvinia, father of Loosh and Simon, grandfather of Ringo, and an old, faithful servant of the Sartoris family. *The Unvanquished,* "Ambuscade," "Retreat," "Raid."

Jock, a pilot in an airplane acrobatic act. A skilled aviator, he toured small towns in an unlicensed plane with his partner Ginsfarb. "Death Drag."

Jody, an employee in Willy Christian's drugstore in Jefferson. *As I Lay Dying.*

Joe, a blind beggar. His wife had a face like that of the Mona Lisa. "Episode."

Joe, a young bootlegger. "Once Aboard the Lugger."

John Henry, a conscientious Negro lad who helped rescue young Bayard Sartoris from his wrecked automobile. *Sartoris.*

John Paul, a Negro servant for a Mottstown family. "That Will Be Fine."

Jonas, a Negro slave who belonged to Buck and Buddy McCaslin. "Was."

Jones, the secretary of the Fair Association. "Death Drag."

Jones, Herschell, a minor suitor of Narcissa Benbow Sartoris. *Sanctuary.*

Jones, Januarius, a fellow of Latin in a small college. "A religio-sentimental orgy in gray tweed, shaping an insincere fleeting articulation of damp clay to an old imperishable desire," this fat sensuous man pursued Cecily Saunders and Emmy and failed with both. Margaret Powers, who thought of him as an "aped intelligence imposed on an innate viciousness," never gave him an opportunity to pursue her. *Soldiers' Pay.*

Jones, Milly (1853–69), the fatherless daughter of a woman who died in a Memphis brothel. A resident of Sutpen's Hundred, with her grandfather, Wash Jones, she served as Thomas Sutpen's "last hope" in establishing his dynasty, a hope bloodily extinguished when her grandfather killed her and her new-born child, a daughter. *Absalom, Absalom!,* "Wash."

Jones, Wash (–1869), the "poor white trash" servant an
long-time companion and supporter of Thomas Sutpen. Afte
twenty years of trying, he got "a holt of old Sutpen at last whei
Sutpen will either have to tear meat or squeal." With a scyth
he destroyed Sutpen, and with a butcher knife slaughtered h
granddaughter, Milly, and new-born great-granddaughter. Twelv
hours after these murders, he was dead, running straight into th
gun barrels of the sheriff's men. *Absalom, Absalom!*, "Wash.

Josh. *See* Robyn, Theodore.

Jubal, a Negro servant of Saucier Weddel. "Mountain Victory.

Julio, a Boston Italian who aimed to charge Quentin Compso
with "meditated criminal assault" of his little sister. *The Soun
and the Fury.*

K

Kauffman, Julius, a Semitic man and brother of Eva Wiseman. H
was a member of the Maurier yachting party, occupied most c
the time with whiskey and conversation. *Mosquitoes.*

Kemp, Beasley, a Yoknapatawpha County horse trader. *The Han
let,* "Fool About a Horse."

Kennedy, Watt, the sheriff of Mottstown in whose charge Jc
Christmas was placed. "A fat, comfortable man with a harc
canny head and a benevolent aspect," he did what he could t
uphold the law against the fanaticism of Percy Grimm and th
almost obscene greed of Lucas Burch. *Light in August.*

Ketcham, the Jefferson jailer. "Pantaloon in Black."

Killebrew, Miss, a teller at Manfred de Spain's bank. *The Towr*

Killegrew, Hampton, the Jefferson night marshal. "Knight
Gambit."

Killegrew, Hunter, a Jefferson deputy who escorted Montgomer
Ward Snopes to Parchman prison. *The Mansion.*

Killegrew, Old Man, a Frenchman's Bend resident who playe
the radio loudly because his wife was deaf. "Two Soldiers,
"Shingles for the Lord."

King, Mrs. Alvina, the mother of Louise King. She was intent o
seeing her only daughter properly married. "Doctor Martino.

King, Louise, born and reared in Mississippi. She developed a strange friendship with Dr. Martino, who taught her that "when you are afraid to do something you know that you are alive." She married Hubert Jarrod. "Doctor Martino."

Kneeland, the proprietor of a tailor and dress-suit rental shop in Jefferson. *The Town.*

Kohl, Barton, a New York sculptor. He married Linda Snopes, and while the couple was fighting for the Loyalist cause in Spain, a period of six months and twenty-nine days, his plane was shot down and he was killed. *The Mansion.*

Kohl, Linda Snopes (April 12, 1908—   ), the Mississippi-born daughter of Hoake McCarron and Eula Varner Snopes. Like her mother, this "young pointer bitch" impressed Gavin Stevens, who wanted to save her from being a Snopes and succeeded in gaining her entrance to the university at Oxford. After her mother's death she was sent by Stevens to live in Greenwich Village, where she met and married Barton Kohl. The pair joined the Loyalist cause in Spain; Kohl was killed, and Linda was deafened as a result of a bomb explosion. After her return to Jefferson she was investigated by the FBI because she was a communist. Despite this she worked valiantly as a riveter in the Pascagoula shipyard during the war. Her intense antipathy to her "father," Flem Snopes, who among other devious schemes had stolen her Communist party card for purposes of blackmail, was revealed in her efforts to get Mink Snopes pardoned, for she suspected Mink's desire for revenge against Flem. *The Town, The Mansion.*

L

Labove, a Mississippi-born schoolteacher. He worked his way through the state university at Oxford by playing football, received a Master of Arts degree and a Bachelor of Laws, and was admitted to the bar. He taught school at Frenchman's Bend for six years, departing suddenly from the area after clumsily failing to seduce reluctant pupil Eula Varner. *The Hamlet.*

Lafe, a hill-country man and frequenter of Will Gibson's country store. "The Liar."

Lafe, the father of Dewey Dell Bundren's unborn child. He gave her ten dollars for an abortion. *As I Lay Dying.*

Lallemont, General, a corps commander in the French Army during World War I. Superior in rank to General Gragnon, he had been a subaltern in the same regiment as Gragnon in their youth. Lallemont had "along with ability just enough of the sort of connections which . . . made the difference between division and corps command. . . ." *A Fable.*

Lamar, Ruby, the common-law wife of bootlegger Lee Goodwin. A sometime waitress and prostitute to earn money for her husband's release from prison, this proud woman and hard-pressed mother of a sickly baby showed Temple Drake what it meant to have "the guts . . . to be in love." *Sanctuary.*

Lapin, a thief with a "swaggering face, reckless and sardonic, incorrigible and debonair." He shared a prison cell in France with Horse and the Corporal and was killed by the same firing squad. According to him, "A man aint even the sum of his vices: just his habits." *A Fable.*

Ledbetter, Mrs., a Rockyford resident. She bought a sewing machine from V. K. Ratliff. *The Mansion.*

Legate, Will, a member of the Carothers Edmonds-Isaac McCaslin hunting party. One of the "finest shots" in the county, he was assigned the job of preventing Lucas Beauchamp from being lynched for the Vinson Gowrie murder. *Intruder in the Dust,* "Delta Autumn," "Race at Morning."

Levine, Gerald David, an eighteen-year-old second lieutenant in the RAF. "Incredulous and amazed," he refused to believe the war could be over before he could prove himself brave and heroic. He would not be the first nor the last to think what he could have done "for motherland's glory had motherland but matched me with her need." *A Fable.*

Levitt, Matt, a twenty-one-year-old garage mechanic, originally from Ohio. An ex-Golden Gloves champion, this mean-mouthed and mean-minded racing driver left Jefferson shortly after a fight with Gavin Stevens, caused by Linda Snopes's obvious preference for Stevens and John Donne's poetry. *The Town.*

Lewis, Matt, owner of a livery stable. *Idyll in the Desert.*

Lilley, a Jefferson resident and shopkeeper who wanted Lucas Beauchamp lynched. *Intruder in the Dust.*

Linscomb, Colonel, the principal citizen of Parsham, Tennessee, and owner of Acheron, the horse competing against the one "owned" by the Hogganbeck-Ned-Lucius Priest trio. *The Reivers.*

Lion, a part Airedale bear dog tamed by Sam Fathers and Boon Hogganbeck, but belonging to Major Cassius de Spain. Lion helped in the killing of Old Ben and was killed himself in the struggle. He was buried in the woods near Sam Fathers. *The Town,* "The Bear."

Little Belle. *See* Mitchell, Belle.

Littlejohn, Mrs., the owner of a Frenchman's Bend boardinghouse through which ran one of Flem Snopes's wild Texas ponies. She was kind to Ike Snopes. *The Hamlet, The Town,* "Lizards in Jamshyd's Courtyard," "Spotted Horses."

Log-in-the-Creek, an Indian who played the harmonica and won Herman Basket's sister. "A Courtship."

Long, Judge, a north Mississippi Federal judge. "He was six and a half feet tall and his nose looked almost a sixth of that." He passed sentence on Wilbur Provine and Montgomery Ward Snopes. *The Town, The Mansion.*

Loosh. *See* Lucius.

Lorraine, Miss, a Memphis prostitute, friend of Reba Rivers, and mourner of Alabama Red. *Sanctuary.*

Louisa, Aunt, the sister of Rodney and George's aunt. During a tearful trip to Mottstown, she ardently defended her brother. "That Will Be Fine."

Louvinia, wife of Joby, mother of Philadelphia, and grandmother of Ringo. *The Unvanquished,* "My Grandmother Millard," "Ambuscade," "Retreat," "Raid."

Lovelady, a widower of a suicide victim. He sold coffin insurance to Jefferson Negroes. "That Evening Sun."

Lovemaiden, Butch, the "Law" from Hardwick. He was out of his bailiwick and in Beat Four when he attempted to debase his police badge by preying on Everbe Corinthia, "the helpless kind," to whom he was attracted. Boon Hogganbeck, Sam Caldwell, and Lucius Priest, as well as most of the people in the Beat, all managed to circumvent his desire. *The Reivers.*

Lowe, Julian, a flying cadet. This nineteen-year-old mother-dominated romantic proposed marriage to Margaret Powers. The war ended two weeks before this "embryonic ace" earned his wings, thereby frustrating his dreams of heroism and wounds. *Soldiers' Pay.*

Lucas. *See* Beauchamp, Lucas.

Lucius (Loosh), the son of Joby, husband of Philadelphia, uncle of Ringo. He proved to be a traitor to his own people as well as to the Sartoris family. *The Unvanquished,* "My Grandmother Millard," "Ambuscade," "Retreat," "Raid."

Ludus, a Negro driver for the Priest livery stable in Jefferson. He was shot at and missed five times from twenty feet away by Boon Hogganbeck. *The Reivers.*

Luster, the son of Frony. A part of the Compson menage, he took care of Benjy Compson, the idiot son. According to his grandmother, Dilsey, he had "jes as much Compson devilment . . . es any of em." *The Sound and the Fury, Absalom, Absalom! The Reivers.*

Lycurgus. *See* Briggins, Lycurgus.

M

MacCallum. *See* McCallum.

McCallum (MacCallum), Anse and Lucius (1920?–), twin sons of Virginius (Buddy) McCallum. They enlisted in the U.S. Army before World War II. *The Town,* "The Tall Men," "Knight's Gambit."

McCallum (MacCallum), Henry, second son of Virginius (old Anse). He did most of the housekeeping for the family. *Sartoris.*

McCallum (MacCallum), Jackson, oldest son of Virginius (old Anse). *Sartoris,* "The Tall Men."

McCallum (MacCallum), Lee, the quiet son of Virginius (old Anse). *Sartoris,* "The Tall Men."

McCallum (MacCallum), Raphael Semmes (1875–), fourth son of Virginius McCallum. He "knew more about horses probably than any man in the country." *Sartoris, The Mansion,* "The Tall Men," "Knight's Gambit."

McCallum (MacCallum), Stuart, son of Virginius (old Anse), twin of Raphael. *Sartoris, As I Lay Dying,* "The

McCallum (MacCallum), Virginius (old Anse) (184
a Yoknapatawpha farmer whose property lay abo
miles from Jefferson. At the age of sixteen, in 1861, ᴵᴵᵉ walked
to Lexington, Virginia to enlist in Stonewall Jackson's army.
After 1865 he walked back to Mississippi, married, fathered six
sons and taught them "honor and pride and discipline that
make a man worth preserving, make him of any value." Chick
Mallison and Gavin Stevens shot quail at the McCallum farm,
and Bayard Sartoris hunted there after he killed his grandfather
in the car wreck. *Sartoris, As I Lay Dying, The Hamlet,* "The
Tall Men."

McCallum (MacCallum), Virginius (Buddy) (1899–   ), son
of Virginius (old Anse) McCallum and father of twin sons,
Anse and Lucius. He brought back two medals from World
War I. When he was in his late thirties he lost his leg in a
hammer mill accident. *Sartoris, The Town,* "The Tall Men."

McCannon, Shreve (Mackenzie), born in Alberta, Canada, he
shared a room at Harvard with Quentin Compson in 1909–10,
and helped reconstruct the story of the Sutpen rise and fall.
The Sound and the Fury, Absalom, Absalom!

McCarron, Hoake, the son of Alison Hoake, from Tennessee. At
age twenty-three, despite a broken arm and considerable competition, this "wild buck" was the first to win Eula Varner's
favor. "He was unbitted not because he was afraid of a bit but
simply because so fur he didn't prefer to be." He departed
hastily from the Yoknapatawpha territory, leaving Eula pregnant. He returned east years later, big, rich and hard, appearing
at his daughter Linda Snopes's wedding to Barton Kohl in New
York. *The Hamlet, The Town, The Mansion.*

McCaslin, Delphine. *See* Delphine.

McCaslin, Amodeus (–*ca.* 1869), son of Lucius Quintus
Carothers McCaslin, and twin of Theophilus McCaslin. Known
familiarly as "Uncle Buddy," he did the housework and cooking
on the plantation, while his twin did the farming. At their
father's death the pair set about arranging for the manumission
of their father's slaves. During the Civil War, although past
seventy, Amodeus served as a sergeant in Tennant's brigade in

Virginia, and later he temporarily saved his brother from marriage to Sophonsiba Beauchamp. *The Unvanquished,* "Was," "The Bear," "Vendée."

McCaslin, Isaac (1867–   ), son of Theophilus (Buck) and Sophonsiba Beauchamp McCaslin, grandson of Lucius Quintus Carothers McCaslin. From early boyhood the woods were "his mistress and his wife" and Sam Fathers was his mentor. He grew to be one of the best hunters in the county and because of his experiences in the woods he, at age twenty-one, relinquished his heritage to McCaslin Edmonds, believing that the land had never rightfully belonged to him or his ancestors. For the next sixty years, even after his marriage in 1895, he lived in a rented room and then in a small house in Jefferson, in the hope that "he could repudiate the wrong and shame, at least in principle." But his real home was the woods in which he spent two weeks each November. *The Town, The Mansion, The Reivers,* "Was," "The Bear," "The Old People," "A Bear Hunt," "Lion," "Delta Autumn," "Fool About a Horse," "Race at Morning," "The Fire and the Hearth."

McCaslin, Lucius Quintus Carothers (1772—June 27, 1837), Carolina-born progenitor of the white McCaslin and Edmonds lines, and the mixed-race Beauchamp line. By his wife he fathered twin sons, Amodeus and Theophilus, and a daughter whose daughter married an Edmonds. By Negress Tomasina (Tomy) he fathered a son, Turl (Terrel), who married a Beauchamp. He made no effort "either to explain or obfuscate the thousand-dollar legacy to the son of an unmarried slave-girl" for "his fame would suffer only after he was no longer present to defend it." *Intruder in the Dust, The Reivers,* "The Fire and the Hearth," "The Bear," "The Old People."

McCaslin, Ned William (1860–   ), the son of the natural daughter of old Lucius Quintus Carothers McCaslin and a Negro slave. Husband of the Priest's cook, Delphine, and coachman for "Boss" Priest, he joined Boon Hogganbeck and young Lucius Priest on their eventful escapade in Memphis. Wise and patient and experienced, he made it clear that he "was a McCaslin." *The Reivers.*

McCaslin, Sophonsiba (Sibbey) Beauchamp, the sister of Hubert

Beauchamp, wife of Theophilus McCaslin. She bore one son, Isaac Beauchamp McCaslin, in 1867. "Was," "The Bear."

McCaslin, Theophilus (–*ca.* 1869), son of Lucius Quintus Carothers McCaslin, and twin of Amodeus. Known familiarly as "Uncle Buck," he ran the plantation and did the farming. At the age of seventy he became a member of Colonel Sartoris' regiment in Forrest's command. Even later in life, after considerable maneuvering by Hubert Beauchamp, Theophilus married Sophonsiba Beauchamp, and to them in 1867 was born a son, Isaac. *Absalom, Absalom!, The Unvanquished, The Hamlet,* "Vendée," "Was," "The Bear," "Retreat."

McCord, a bachelor friend of Charlotte Rittenmeyer and Harry Wilbourne. He worked for a Chicago paper. *The Wild Palms.*

McEachern, Mr. and Mrs., a farm couple. A rugged and ruthless Presbyterian fanatic, Simon McEachern adopted five-year-old Joe Christmas from a Memphis orphanage, determined to teach him "to fear God and abhor idleness and vanity despite his origin." His wife, "a patient, beaten creature without sex demarcation at all save the neat screw of graying hair and the skirt," was as kind as she could be to the boy and offered affection which he would not accept. When Christmas was about eighteen, he stole her small reserve of money, murdered McEachern, and fled. *Light in August.*

McGinnis, Darrel, a lieutenant in the Air Force during World War I. He and Captain Bogard thought they were showing the English boy something of the war. "Turnabout."

MacGowan (McGowan), Skeet (Skeets), a clerk and soda jerker in Uncle Willy Christian's drugstore. He responded to Dewey Dell Bundren's request for abortive pills by seducing her. *As I Lay Dying, The Town, The Mansion.*

McKellogg, Colonel and Mrs., an army couple stationed in Memphis who bought dinner for the young Grier boy. "Two Soldiers."

McLendon, Jackson, the organizer and captain of the Sartoris Rifles, U.S. Army, during World War I. *Light in August, The Town, The Mansion.*

McLendon, John, a Jefferson resident who led the lynching of Will Mayes. "Dry September."

McNamara, a New Orleans petty race-track swindler and putative jockey. He was a partner of Morowitz. "Damon and Pythias Unlimited."

McWilliams, a train conductor. "Knight's Gambit."

McWillie, the son of Colonel Linscomb's chauffeur. He was the jockey for Acheron in the hotly contested races at Parsham, Tennessee. *The Reivers.*

MacWyrglinchbeath, a first-class air mechanic in the RAF during World War I. This incredible miser was once guilty of simultaneous desertion from two different military units. "Thrift."

Madden, Rufus, a sergeant in World War I, present when Richard Powers was shot at point-blank range. *Soldiers' Pay.*

Magda. *See* Marthe.

Mahon, Donald (—May, 1919), an RAF hero in World War I, winner of a Purple Heart. He returned to his Georgia home town to collect his soldier's pay: the fact that his fiancée, Cecily Saunders, was no longer interested. Badly scarred and blind, he remembered nothing that had happened before he was wounded. Before he died he married Margaret Powers. *Soldiers' Pay.*

Mahon, Reverend Joseph, the Episcopal rector of Charlestown, Georgia. A big, mild-mannered man, father of Lieutenant Donald Mahon, he hopefully avoided acknowledgment of his son's fate. Believing that he had "never been able to do anything well" except to raise flowers, he "had thought to grow old with my books among my roses." *Soldiers' Pay.*

Mahon, Margaret Powers, a twenty-four-year-old war widow. She was twice tricked by "a wanton fate": her first husband, Lieutenant Richard Powers, with whom she had spent three days, was killed in France; her second husband, Lieutenant Donald Mahon, whom she and Joe Gilligan picked up and cared for during his final months, died from his war wounds a few weeks after she married him. After Mahon's death, she refused Gilligan's marriage proposal because she did not have "the courage to risk it again." *Soldiers' Pay.*

Mallison, Charles, a Jefferson resident. Husband of Margaret and father of Charles (Chick), he remained largely in the background, overshadowed by his brother-in-law, Gavin Stevens. *Intruder in the Dust, The Town.*

Mallison, Charles (Chick) (November 11, 1913, according to

The Town; 1914, according to *The Mansion;* 1922 or 1923, according to "Knight's Gambit"—   ), the Jefferson-born son of Charles and Margaret Stevens Mallison. He graduated from Harvard in June, 1938, served in the war as a bombardier, was a prisoner of war, and returned in September, 1945, to re-enter Harvard for his M.A. and law degrees (according to *The Mansion*). He attended the Jefferson Academy, was first in his class, and left as a cadet lieutenant-colonel in the ROTC to join the service in World War II (according to "Knight's Gambit"). The nephew of Gavin Stevens, Chick played his major role in *Intruder in the Dust* as the new hope of the rising generation in the South, heeding his uncle's advice: "Some things you must never stop refusing to bear. Injustice and outrage and dishonor and shame." *Intruder in the Dust, The Town, The Mansion,* "Tomorrow," "Knight's Gambit," "An Error in Chemistry," "By the People," "The Waifs."

Mallison, Margaret (1889–   ), the wife of Charles Mallison, twin sister of Gavin Stevens, mother of Chick. She aided her son and brother in the protection of accused murderer Lucas Beauchamp. Of her Chick said, "If dentist's drills could talk, that's exactly what Mother would have sounded like." Her brother said of her that she had tried to be his mother ever since theirs had died, and "someday she may succeed." *Intruder in the Dust, Requiem for a Nun, The Town, The Mansion.*

Mandy, a Negro cook at McCallum's. *Sartoris.*

Mannigoe, Nancy, a Negress of about thirty. She was for a time the domestic servant of Gowan and Temple Drake Stevens. Previously, this tall woman "with a calm impenetrable almost bemused face" had been a cook, a cotton chopper, a dope addict, and a prostitute. To prevent the dissolution of the Stevens marriage, she murdered their baby daughter. She was tried, convicted, and hanged in the town of Jefferson. *See* Nancy. *Requiem for a Nun.*

Marders, Mrs. Sarah, a friend of Belle Mitchell. *Sartoris.*

Markey, Robert, a Memphis lawyer and city politician. He formed a friendship with Gavin Stevens at Heidelberg. "Knight's Gambit."

Marshal (Generalissimo, Old General), chief of the High Command in France during World War I. The nephew of a cabinet minister, godson of the board chairman of a gigantic munitions federation, an orphan, the last male of his line, "his was the golden destiny of an hereditary crown prince of paradise." He attended St. Cyr Academy, was graduated top in the class, and served France from Brazzaville to Saigon, rising steadily to become Number One "among all the desperate and allied peoples in Western Europe." He was a "slight gray man with a face wise, intelligent, and unbelieving, who no longer believed in anything but his disillusion and his intelligence and his limitless power." The Corporal was his son who must die by his order, because this had been "bequeathed to him at birth." When he himself died, the day "was gray, as though in dirge for him to whom it owed for the right and privilege to mourn in peace without terror or concern." A *Fable*.

Marthe (Magda), reared near Beirut, the sister of Marya, half-sister of the Corporal. As a youngster, at the death in childbirth of her stepmother, she acted as the "mother of two—the infant brother and the idiot sister two years her senior." She married a French soldier who had a farm near St. Mihiel. Iron-faced and strong, she came to realize that she had no right to "demand uniqueness for grieving" and that "work is the only anesthetic to which grief is vulnerable." With her sister and sister-in-law, she traveled with her brother's body to bury it in its temporary resting place on the farm. A *Fable*.

Martino, Jules, a St. Louis heart specialist and bachelor. His heart condition forced him to retire and he spent his last days developing a strange friendship with young Louise King. "Doctor Martino."

Mary, a young girl whom Johnny Gray protected from the "Wop." For Johnny, she turned into "little Sister Death." "The Kid Learns."

Marya (Dumont), sister of Marthe. Her husband died the last year of World War I, because he "probably decided that he could not bear another peace." Of her half-brother, the Corporal, she said, "He did the best he could, all he could, and now he doesn't need to worry any more. Now all he has to do is rest." Serene and gentle, she had "the peaceful face of the witless." A *Fable*.

Matron, the unnamed directoress of the Memphis orphanage in which Joe Christmas was placed. He had been left there by his grandfather, Eupheus Hines. "Past fifty, flabby faced, with weak, kind frustrated eyes," she was appalled at the suggestion that the boy had Negro blood. *Light in August.*

Maurier, Mrs. Patricia, a wealthy widow of a not quite acceptable southerner. She was the aunt of Pat and Theodore Robyn and "went through the world continually amazed at chance, whether or not she had instigated it." She was far more tolerant of artists than they were of her. *Mosquitoes.*

Maxey, the owner and manager of a Jefferson barber shop. "Hair."

Maydew, a Jefferson sheriff who helped bring in the murderer, Rider. "Pantaloon in Black."

Mayes, Will, the Negro night watchman at the ice plant. He was accused of rape by Minnie Cooper, and lynched by a Jefferson mob. "Dry September."

Meadowfill, a Jefferson resident who held "the top name for curmudgeonry." A retired old miser, he spent his declining years making life a living hell for his daughter, Essie, cursing at stray dogs and small boys who crossed his property, and carrying on an active shot-gun feud with Orestes Snopes and his hogs. His unsympathetic neighbors believed that "if he didn't look out that window some morning and see a hog in his orchard, he would die of simply hope unbearably deferred." *The Mansion.*

Meadowfill, Essie. *See* Smith, Essie Meadowfill.

Meek, Melissa, the Jefferson librarian, a spinster. Mouse-sized and mouse-colored, she went to school with Candace Compson. *The Sound and the Fury.*

Merridew, Mrs., a Jefferson do-gooder. She became Willy Christian's guardian and trustee, contributed a large share to Willy's torment, and capped her "helpful" activities by having him committed to the Keeley asylum. "Uncle Willy."

Metcalf, a Mottstown deputy. *Light in August.*

Midgleston, Wilfred, a one-time New York architect's draftsman. At age fifty-six, after a harrowing day as Pan, he left his home and wife Martha, and spent the rest of his life as a penniless bum in Rincon, Mexico. "Black Music."

Millard, Rosa, the mother-in-law of Colonel John Sartoris, grandmother of Bayard. Her delightfully underhanded efforts on behalf of the Confederacy were brought to a shocking end by the treachery of Ab Snopes and Major Grumby. *The Unvanquished, The Hamlet,* "Vendée," "The Unvanquished," "My Grandmother Millard," "Ambuscade," "Retreat," "Raid."

Miller, a Jefferson citizen who taught the men's Bible class. He, too, tried to "save" Uncle Willy Christian. "Uncle Willy."

Milly. *See* Jones, Milly.

Minnie, a Negro servant with a fabulous gold tooth. She worked at Reba Rivers' house of prostitution in Memphis. Under orders from Popeye Vitelli she guarded Temple Drake after Temple had been brought to the house. *Sanctuary, The Mansion, The Reivers.*

Mitchell, Belle, the daughter of Harry and Belle Mitchell, stepdaughter of Horace Benbow. She was a creature of "pure dissimulation" whose welfare occupied more of her step-father's thoughts than those of her mother. *Sartoris, Sanctuary.*

Mitchell, Mrs. Belle. *See* Benbow, Belle Mitchell.

Mitchell, Harry, a Jefferson cotton speculator. He was married to Belle and was the father of Little Belle. He left his wife when he discovered that she was in love with Horace Benbow. *Sartoris.*

Mitchell, Hugh, a Frenchman's Bend resident and gallery-sitter at the Whiteleaf Store. *The Hamlet.*

Mohataha, the mother of Ikkemotubbe, sister of old Issetibbeha. *Requiem for a Nun.*

Moketubbe, the son of Issetibbeha. A gross figure, "diseased with flesh," he succeeded his father as chieftain of the Chickasaws, but following the death of his eight-year-old son and the return of Ikkemotubbe, he abdicated. *Big Woods,* "Red Leaves," "The Old People."

Monaghan, the son of an Irish immigrant. Educated at Yale, he served in the RAF during World War I as part of Bridesman's Flight B. He went two thousand miles to kill Huns so that he could "get to hell back home." *A Fable,* "Ad Astra," "Honor."

Monckton, a shipmate of George and Carl. He was an observer of and commentator on their strange relationship. "Divorce in Naples."

Monk. *See* Odlethrop, Stonewall Jackson.

Montgomery, Jake, a "shoestring timber-buyer from Crossman County." At one time he ran a restaurant near Memphis. He became implicated in the timber swindle of Crawford Gowrie in Beat Four. The "price of his silence" resulted in his own murder. *Intruder in the Dust.*

Mooney, the foreman at the Jefferson planing mill. *Light in August.*

Morache, one of the twelve mutineers on the French front in 1918. He had a valuable watch with a Swiss movement, stolen from the body of a German colonel whom Morache had murdered while on patrol to bring back a prisoner. In exchange for this watch, the sit-down group was given a corpse to replace the one they had originally chosen for the Tomb of the Unknown Soldier. *A Fable.*

Morowitz, a Jewish petty swindler and race track tout in New Orleans. "Damon and Pythias Unlimited."

Moseley, a druggist in Mottstown from whom Dewey Dell Bundren tried to buy abortion pills. *As I Lay Dying.*

Mothershed, an atheist friend of Judge Allison. He ended his life by suicide. "Beyond."

Myrtle, Miss, a Memphis prostitute, friend of Reba Rivers, and mourner of Alabama Red. *Sanctuary.*

N

Nancy, a Negro laundress employed for a short time by the Compson family. Her prostitution resulted in her getting her teeth kicked out by Mr. Stovall, her attempted suicide, and, finally her murder by her husband, Jesus. (In *Faulkner in the University,* the author states that this Nancy and Nancy Mannigoe are "the same person, actually," p. 79.) "That Evening Sun."

Nancy. *See* Mannigoe, Nancy.

Nat. *See* Wilkins, Nat Beauchamp.

Ned. *See* McCaslin, Ned William.

Nelson, Caroline, an old Negro woman. She was Donald Mahon's "mammy." *Soldiers' Pay.*

Nelson, Loosh, the grandson of Caroline (Aunt Callie) Nelson.

He served as a corporal in the army during World War I. *Soldiers' Pay.*

Nightingale, Mr., a Jefferson cobbler who believed "that Lee had betrayed the whole South when he surrendered at Appomattox" and who threw out his son when the boy joined the U.S. Army. *The Mansion.*

Nightingale, Tug, the bachelor son of a Hard-Shell Baptist cobbler. Tug was "an homme fatal" to mules and "a standard-type provincial county-seat house painter" until the U.S. declared war. Defying his fanatic father by joining the army to which Lee had betrayed the South, he was the first Yoknapatawpha County soldier to go overseas and among the last to return, in late 1919. *The Mansion.*

Nunnery, Cedric, a five-year-old boy for whom Eck Snopes gave his life when the mother reported Cedric lost near the oil tank. *The Town.*

O

Odlethrop, Stonewall Jackson (Monk), a semimoronic Yoknapatawpha resident. He murdered his grandmother, was later sent to prison for another murder, and finally was hanged for the murder of the warden. "Monk."

Odum, Cliff, the Frenchman's Bend resident who helped Vynie Snopes get her separator. *The Hamlet.*

Old Anse. *See* McCallum, Virginius (Old Anse).

Old Ben, the bear. Like Sam Fathers and Lion, Old Ben was "taintless and incorruptible." According to Sam, in order to get Old Ben a man "will need to be just a little bigger than smart, and a little braver than either." "The Bear."

Old Het, a poorhouse resident. At seventy, she was "tall, lean, fogheaded, in tennis shoes and a long rat-colored cloak trimmed with what forty or fifty years ago had been fur." She frequently visited Mrs. Mannie Hait. *The Town,* "Mule in the Yard."

Old Man Anse. *See* Holland, Anselm.

Old Man Ash. *See* Wylie, Old Man Ash.

Ord, Matt, a resident of New Valois, Louisiana. He held the world's speed record for the land plane. He was cajoled into selling his ship to Roger Shumann after Shumann's own plane was wrecked the day before the major race. *Pylon.*

Otis, the nephew of Everbe Corinthia (Miss Corrie). He came from Arkansas to visit her in Memphis for some "refinement." According to Lucius Priest, "there was something wrong about him." That "something" was that he looked eleven but was actually fifteen, and had the morals of a shark. *The Reivers.*

Otto, a New Orleans thug and friend of Johnny Gray. "The Kid Learns."

Owl-By-Night, a young Indian. "A Courtship."

P

Painter, a ranch owner. *Idyll in the Desert.*

Pap, an old man cared for by Lee Goodwin and Ruby Lamar at their near-Jefferson bootlegging headquarters. He was blind and deaf. *Sanctuary.*

Patterson, Mr. and Mrs., the Jefferson neighbors of the Compson family. Patterson was suspicious, with good reason, of his wife's relationship with Maury Bascomb, the brother of Caroline Compson. *The Sound and the Fury.*

Paul (The Breton), second in command of the squad of twelve mutineers during World War I in France. He was a "squat powerful weathered man with the blue eyes and reddish hair and beard of a Breton fisherman." *A Fable.*

Peabody, Lucius Quintus (1832–   ), medical successor to Dr. Habersham. A fabulously long-lived Jefferson physician, stout of heart and body, familiarly called "Loosh," he was an essential element of the Yoknapatawpha scene. His son, also a physician, and called "young Loosh," lived in New York City. *Sartoris, As I Lay Dying, The Hamlet, Requiem for a Nun, The Town, The Reivers,* "Beyond," "The Waifs."

Pearson, a state draft investigator. He wanted to arrest Anse and Lucius McCallum, but their father sent them away to enlist. "The Tall Men."

Pete, a friend of Jean-Baptiste. "Home."

Pete, the brother of Alabama Red. He was blackmailing Temple Drake Stevens with some passionate letters she had written to his brother. After several meetings, he and Temple planned to run off, but were prevented from doing so by the murder of Temple's baby daughter. *Requiem for a Nun.*

Pete, the younger brother of Joe, a bootlegger. "Once Aboard the Lugger."

Pettigrew, the Jefferson mortician who buried Judge Howard Allison. "Beyond."

Pettigrew, Thomas Jefferson, the pony express rider of settlement days. Jefferson was named after him. *Requiem for a Nun.*

Philadelphy, the daughter of Louvinia, wife of Lucius (Loosh). She was a Sartoris servant. When Loosh deserted the Sartoris family during the Civil War, she followed him because he was her husband. *The Unvanquished,* "My Grandmother Millard," "Ambuscade," "Retreat."

Philip, a young Jefferson bank cashier engaged to Elly. "Elly"

Picklock, one of the squad of twelve mutineers on the French front in 1918. He had been "a fairly successful picklock in civilian life before 1914," and planned to return to that vocation. After the Corporal's death, he and the remaining members were assigned the task of choosing "one complete cadaver of one French soldier unidentified and unidentifiable" to be placed in the Tomb of the Unknown Soldier. *A Fable.*

Pinckski, a New Yorker. He sold coffin insurance to Mrs. Margaret Noonan Gihon. "Pennsylvania Station."

Polchek, the traitor among the squad of twelve supporting the Corporal's mutiny in 1918 in France. With "a knowing, almost handsome metropolitan face" he sat at the Corporal's right during the last meal in prison, not eating or drinking. For his information, he was promised brandy and thirty coins, the only money he ever "earned by honest sweat." *A Fable.*

Poleymus, the constable of Beat Four. During the complexities resulting from the Lightning-Acheron horse race and the intrusion of policeman Butch Lovemaiden on the scene, he maintained his status coolly and firmly. *The Reivers.*

Popeye. *See* Vitelli, Popeye.

Potter, Jack, a New Orleans jockey. Wearing a girl's garter on his arm helped him to win a race. "Cheest."

Powell, John, the head hostler in Maury Priest's livery stable in Jefferson. *The Reivers.*

Powers, Margaret. *See* Mahon, Margaret Powers.

Powers, Richard, a platoon commander during World War I. Three days before he sailed for France he married Margaret. Admittedly not in love with each other, they wanted "to get all the fun" they could. He was killed by one of his own men as he tried to bring order to the "demoralized troops caught in a pointless hysteria" through fear of gas in the trenches. *Soldiers' Pay.*

Priest, Alexander and Lessep, younger brothers of Lucius. *The Reivers.*

Priest, Alison Lessep, the wife of Maury Priest, and mother of four sons. *The Reivers.*

Priest, Lucius (1894–   ), the eldest son of Maury and Alison Lessep Priest, grandson of Lucius (Boss) Priest. When eleven, in the company of Boon Hogganbeck and Ned, he set off in his grandfather's "borrowed" Winton Flyer for a series of adventures which included a night in a Memphis "house of pleasure," encounters with the law, several fantastic race heats atop a sardine-loving race horse, and the formation of a firm friendship with a reformed prostitute. He learned that "a gentleman accepts the responsibility of his actions and bears the burden of their consequences. . . ." *The Reivers.*

Priest, Lucius (Boss) (*ca.* 1850–   ), born in Carolina. He was too young to serve in the Civil War during which his father, a color sergeant for Wade Hampton, was killed in action. In 1864 his mother died, and the following year he arrived in Mississippi to look for his kinsmen. He found and married one of them, Sarah Edmonds, in 1869. To them was born a son, Maury. President of the oldest bank in Jefferson, he and the town's other bank president, Colonel Sartoris, shared an intense disdain for automobiles, but because Sartoris passed a decree against their use in Jefferson, Priest felt it necessary to abrogate such a decree in order to maintain his own position as senior citizen in town. *The Reivers.*

Priest, Maury, son of Lucius (Boss) Priest, husband of Alison, and father of four sons: Lucius, Lessep, Maury, and Alexander. He was owner of the livery stable in Jefferson. *The Reivers.*

Priest, Sally Hampton, a Jefferson girl. She turned down Grenier Weddel to marry Maurice Priest. *The Town.*

Priest, Sarah, "a McCaslin, too," the wife of Lucius (Boss) Priest, and grandmother of young Lucius. *The Reivers.*

Pritchel, Ellie. *See* Flint, Ellie Pritchel.

Pritchel, Wesley, a Yoknapatawpha County farmer and widower. He outlived four of his children but was murdered by his son-in-law, Joel Flint. "An Error in Chemistry."

Provine, Lucius (Butch), one-time distiller and leader of the so-called Provine Gang. The group engaged in such vicious practical jokes as burning the celluloid collars of worshippers at a Negro religious meeting. Years later this prank was avenged by Old Man Ash Wylie. "A Bear Hunt," "Dry September."

Provine, Wilbur, a Frenchman's Bend distiller. He was sentenced by Judge Long to the state penitentiary for five years "not for making whiskey, but for letting his wife carry water a mile and a half from that spring." *The Town.*

Pruitt, the president of the Compress Association in Mottstown. "That Will Be Fine."

Pruitt, Rufus, a farmer neighbor of Stonewall Jackson Fentry. "Tomorrow."

Q

Quartermaster General, a French high official during World War I. He was Number Two at St. Cyr Academy and closest friend to Number One, the Marshal. "A man without family or influence or money," he had nothing "save the dubious capacity . . . to endure." After three years as Quartermaster General, he tried to resign following the mutiny and the taking of the German general, for he had lost faith in the man he loved, the Marshal, thinking he had betrayed mankind and its hopes for peace. *A Fable.*

Quick, Ben, the father of Isham Quick. A Frenchman's Bend sawmill owner, he sold his goats to Flem Snopes. *The Hamlet,* "Tomorrow."

Quick, Isham, the son of Ben Quick. Isham was first to arrive on the scene of the Buck Thorpe murder. "Tomorrow."

Quick, Solon (Lon), a Frenchman's Bend resident, farmer, and constable. *As I Lay Dying, The Hamlet, The Mansion,* "Spotted Horses," "Shingles for the Lord," "Lizards in Jamshyd's Courtyard," "Shall Not Perish."

Quick, Theron, the most unlucky of the Frenchman's Bend young bloods eager for Eula Varner. He received for his efforts a "loaded buggy whip across the back of his skull" and was laid out cold in the weeds. He left town "suddenly overnight." *The Mansion.*

Quinn, Dr., a Memphis physician called in by Reba Rivers to treat Temple Drake. *Sanctuary.*

Quistenberry, Dink, a Frenchman's Bend resident. He married a relative of Flem Snopes and moved to Jefferson to take over the Snopes Hotel. "He was the kind of man it just didn't occur to you to say Mister to." *The Town,* "The Waifs."

R

Rachel, one of the best cooks in Jefferson. She worked for the Mitchells. *Sartoris.*

Rachel, wife of Samson. They were neighbors to the Bundrens. *As I Lay Dying.*

Rachel, Aunt, the putative mother of Jesus, who was the husband of Nancy. "That Evening Sun."

Ratliff, Vladimir Kyrlytch (V. K. Ratliffe or V. K. Suratt), a sewing machine agent with headquarters in Jefferson. Despite his first names which "he had to spend half his life trying to live down," he was descended from a long line of fighters, the first of whom was with General John Burgoyne in the Revolution. A confidant of Gavin Stevens, Ratliff devoted all his time to people, and in particular to the Snopes tribe. He "never forgot a name and he knew everyone, man mule and dog, within 50 miles." Shrewd, serene, and able, he was foiled only once: "couldn't nobody but Flem Snopes have foiled Ratliff." *Sartoris, As I Lay Dying, The Hamlet, Requiem for a Nun, The Town, The Mansion,* "A Bear Hunt," "Centaur in Brass," "Lizards in Jamshyd's Courtyard," "By the People," "The Waifs."

Red (**Alabama**), a bouncer employed by Popeye Vitelli in the nightclub near Memphis and encouraged by him to make love to Temple Drake. He was murdered by Popeye behind Reba Rivers' house in Memphis. *Sanctuary, Requiem for a Nun.*

Redlaw. *See* Redmond, Benjamin J.

Redmond, Benjamin J., a Jefferson attorney, the town's "domesticated carpetbagger." He was at one time the railroad partner of John Sartoris. The partnership and any other relationship between the two ended because of Sartoris' "violent and ruthless dictatorialness and will to dominate," and Redmond's ability to "bear and bear and bear until something broke in him," and he killed Sartoris. Later he was confronted by John's son, Bayard, but when the young man refused to shoot, Redmond left Jefferson forever. *Sartoris, The Unvanquished, Requiem for a Nun.*

Reed, Susan. *See* Stribling, Susan Reed.

Reporter, a New Valois (New Orleans) resident. This unnamed man, tall, lean, and sensitive, was sporadically employed by a long-suffering New Orleans newspaper editor, and became almost inextricably involved with the chaotic lives of the flying Shumanns and Jack Holmes. *Pylon.*

Riddell, a Jefferson highway engineer. His son contracted polio. *The Town.*

Rideout, Dr., a physician called to treat Molly Beauchamp. "The Fire and the Hearth."

Rideout, Aaron, a cousin of V. K. Ratliff, and half-owner of a Jefferson restaurant. *The Hamlet.*

Rider, the head of a Jefferson sawmill gang. A big, powerful Negro of twenty-four, he was unable to accept the death of his adored wife, Mannie, six months after their marriage. Crazed with grief and drink, he cut the throat of Birdsong, a white mill worker who had been running a crooked dice game in the mill for fifteen years. After breaking out of the jail, Rider was caught and lynched by Birdsong's relatives. "Pantaloon in Black."

Rider, Mannie, the dead wife of sawmill gang leader Rider. The evening of the day she was buried, a figure resembling her appeared in the Rider home. "Pantaloon in Black."

Ringo (Marengo) (September, 1849—   ), the son of Simon. Close companion of Bayard Sartoris, this intelligent Negro shared Bayard's experiences. *The Unvanquished,* "Vendée," "My Grandmother Millard," "Ambuscade," "Retreat," "Raid."

Rittenmeyer, Charlotte, wife of "Rat" Rittenmeyer and mother of two. It was love at first sight when she met Henry Wilbourne at a party, and for him she deserted family and home. A sculptor of sorts, she supported herself and Wilbourne until he found a semimedical job. Grimly determined to keep their relationship at fever pitch, she argued, "I like bitching and making things with my hands. I don't think that's too much to be permitted to like, to want to have and keep." She died from an illegal abortion, insisted upon by her, and bungled by her lover. *The Wild Palms.*

Rittenmeyer, Francis (Rat), husband of Charlotte and father of two girls. A well-to-do Catholic businessman and resident of New Orleans, this "senior living ex-freshman of the University of Alabama" was jarred from his comfortable existence by his wife's explosive affair with Henry Wilbourne. *The Wild Palms.*

Rivers, Lee, a powdered dandy of Charlestown, Ga. *Soldiers' Pay.*

Rivers, Reba, proprietor of a "dingy three-storey" house of prostitution in Memphis. A big woman who "looked mature . . . in anything," she would "look motherly even while she was throwing out a drunk." Her tenderest thoughts were directed toward her "man" Mr. Binford, dead for two years, her two dogs named Mr. Binford and Miss Reba, and four children, not her own, whom she supported on an Arkansas farm. It was to her house that various Yoknapatawpha citizens came, including Temple Drake, Clarence Snopes, Virgil Snopes, Fonzo Winbush, Boon Hogganbeck, and Lucius Priest. *Sanctuary, The Mansion, The Reivers.*

Robyn, Patricia (Gus), the eighteen-year-old niece of Mrs. Maurier. She and her twin brother, Theodore, were a light-hearted, light-witted pair eager for experience. *Mosquitoes.*

Robyn, Theodore (Josh), the twin brother of Patricia Robyn. A prospective Yale student, he spent his quiet moments carving pipes and looking contemplative. *Mosquitoes.*

Rodney, the uncle of George. To get money, "he tried every known plan except work." He robbed his own parents and his employer, Mr. Pruitt. He was killed by the irate husbands of Mottstown after an attempt to run away with Mrs. Tucker. "That Will Be Fine."

Roebuck, John Wesley, a childhood friend of Charles Mallison. *The Town.*

Rogers, Howard, a pilot for a barn-storming circus. "Honor."

Rogers, Ken, the sheriff at Mitchell. "The Liar."

Rogers, Mildred, the wife of Howard Rogers and mother of one son. She fell in love with Monaghan. "Honor."

Rosie, the Negro cook for George's family in Jefferson. A Dilsey-like character, she was the only one who saw through George. "That Will Be Fine."

Roskus, the mate of Dilsey, and servant of the Compson family. *The Sound and the Fury,* "A Justice."

Roskus (–1841), a Carolina slave brought by Lucius McCaslin to Mississippi, freed on June 27, 1837, but refused to leave, and died January 12, 1841. He was married to Fibby, and they were the parents of Thucydus. "The Bear."

Roskus, Eunice (–1832), a slave bought in 1807 for $650 by Lucius McCaslin. She married Thucydus in 1809 and gave birth, in 1810, to Tomasina, fathered by Lucius McCaslin. On Christmas, 1832, six months before the birth of the son of Tomasina and old McCaslin, Eunice "in formal and succinct repudiation of grief and despair" walked into the creek and drowned herself. "The Bear."

Roskus, Fibby (—August 1, 1849), a Carolina-born slave of Lucius McCaslin who brought her to Mississippi. She was the wife of Roskus, and mother of Thucydus. "The Bear."

Roskus, Thucydus (1779—February 17, 1854), the Carolina-born son of Roskus and Fibby, owned by Lucius McCaslin. He refused offers of land and money from Amodeus and Theophilus McCaslin in 1837, but accepted money in 1841 to set up a blacksmith shop. He married Eunice in 1809. "The Bear."

Ross, Martha, a friend of Howard and Amy Boyd. "The Brooch."

Rouncewell, the oil company agent in Jefferson. *The Reivers.*

Rouncewell, Mrs., the owner of a Jefferson boardinghouse which she and her husband preferred to call the Commercial Hotel. They were eliminated from their ownership by Flem Snopes soon after his return from his wedding trip to Texas. *The Mansion,* "Tomorrow."

Rouncewell, Mrs., proprietor of the Jefferson flower shop. According to Gavin Stevens she ran it not "because she loved flowers nor even money but because she loved funerals." *The Town.*

Runner, a private in a British battalion during World War I. He had once been an officer, but could not face the power which that position entailed and wanted to "get back into the muck" with the men. He died in a "rush of flame which enveloped his body neatly from heel through navel through chin" while trying to organize a mass mutiny before the high command of both sides could learn what the threat was and "start the war again." *A Fable.*

Russell, a Mottstown deputy. *Light in August.*

Russell, Ab, a farmer near Jefferson. *The Sound and the Fury.*

Rust, Everbe Corinthia, an English girl who fell in love with George and stayed in love with his ghost. "The Leg."

Rust, Jotham, the brother of Everbe. During World War I he was arraigned before a court-martial for desertion. "The Leg."

Rust, Simon, the father of Everbe and Jotham Rust. He pulled George out of the Thames. "The Leg."

Ryan, Mrs., the wife of a New Orleans policeman. "The Kid Learns."

S

Samson, and wife Rachel, residents of Frenchman's Bend. Neighbors of the Bundrens, they befriended the family on its hectic burial journey. Samson was convinced that "the best way to respect" Addie Bundren, who had been dead in a box for four days, "is to get her into the ground as quick as you can." *As I Lay Dying.*

Sander, Aleck (Alexander), the son of Paralee (Guster, according to *The Town*). He and Charles Mallison were the same age; the boys were reared together and became fast friends, sharing meals, beds, and adventures. *Intruder in the Dust, The Town.*

Sartoris, Bayard (1840?–62), brother of Colonel John Sartoris and Virginia Sartoris Du Pre. He was killed prior to the second battle of Manassas. *Sartoris, The Unvanquished.*

Sartoris, Bayard (March 16, 1893—June 11, 1920), the son of John and Lucy Cranston Sartoris, and twin of John. After attending the University of Virginia, he married Caroline White in 1917, only to lose her in childbirth in October, 1918. After serving in the Royal Flying Corps and seeing his brother shot down over enemy lines, he returned to Jefferson and married Narcissa Benbow. Seemingly anxious for his own death, he bought a car and raced around the countryside with either his eighty-year-old Aunt Jenny Du Pre or his grandfather, Bayard Sartoris, as passengers. When the car finally crashed, the grandfather died of a heart attack. Young Bayard's life ended in Ohio when the plane he was testing went down on June 11, 1920, the same day Narcissa gave birth to his son Benbow. *Sartoris, The Hamlet, The Mansion,* "Ad Astra."

Sartoris, Colonel Bayard (September, 1849—December, 1919), son of Colonel John Sartoris. As a youngster, aided by Ringo, he tracked down the murderer of his grandmother Rosa Millard. When his father was killed by Benjamin Redmond, he knew he could not live with himself if he took revenge. After studying law at the state university at Oxford, he returned to Jefferson to become one of its leading citizens, its mayor, and president of a bank. In refusing to permit the operation of automobiles on the Jefferson streets, although he died in one driven by his grandson, Bayard, he upheld the Sartoris code, for the "Sartorises differed from other people (who loved themselves first, and knew it secretly) in that they didn't even know they loved themselves first." *The Unvanquished, The Mansion,* "The Bear," "Vendée," "Skirmish at Sartoris," "A Rose for Emily," "Ambuscade," "Retreat," "Raid."

Sartoris, Benbow (Bory) (June 11, 1920—   ), the son of Bayard and Narcissa Benbow Sartoris. Jenny Du Pre insisted on calling him Johnny, after his uncle who had been killed in

France. He served in England during World War II. *Sartoris,
Sanctuary,* "Knight's Gambit," "There Was a Queen."

Sartoris, Caroline White (—October 27, 1918), the first wife
of young Bayard Sartoris. She died in childbirth. *Sartoris.*

Sartoris, Drusilla Hawk (1841–   ), the daughter of Louisa
Hawk, who was a cousin of the late wife of Colonel John
Sartoris. When her fiancé, Gavin Breckbridge, was killed at
Shiloh, she joined Colonel Sartoris' troop of raiders "not to find
a man but to hurt Yankees." After the war she was shamed into
marriage to Colonel Sartoris, and after his murder she left
Mississippi to live with her brother Dennison Hawk in Mont-
gomery. *The Unvanquished,* "Skirmish at Sartoris," "Raid."

Sartoris, John (1823—September 4, 1876), a Confederate colonel
and leading citizen of Jefferson. In 1861, with Thomas Sutpen,
he raised his own independent regiment and "stood in the first
Confederate uniform the town had ever seen." The son-in-law
of Rosa Millard, father of Bayard and two daughters (born 1847
and 1852), in 1865 he married Drusilla Hawk, the daughter of
his first wife's cousin. A long-standing feud with his one-time
friend and partner, Benjamin Redmond (Redlaw, according to
Sartoris) was terminated with the colonel's murder by Redmond. *Sartoris, Absalom, Absalom!, The Unvanquished, Requiem for a Nun,* "My Grandmother Millard," "Vendée," "The
Unvanquished," "Ambuscade," "Retreat."

Sartoris, John (–1901), son of Colonel Bayard Sartoris, husband of Lucy Cranston, and father of twin sons, John and
Bayard. He fought in the Spanish-American War and "suc-
cumbed to yellow fever and an old Spanish bullet-wound."
Sartoris.

Sartoris, John (March 16, 1893—July 5, 1918), son of John and
Lucy Cranston Sartoris, twin of Bayard. He attended the University of Virginia and Princeton before joining the Royal Air
Force in World War I. He "managed to shoot down three huns"
before he himself was shot down and killed over the enemy's
lines. *Sartoris, The Mansion,* "All the Dead Pilots," "Ad
Astra."

Sartoris, Narcissa Benbow (1893–   ), the second wife of Bayard
Sartoris, married in 1919, and the mother of Benbow, named

so by her in the dim hope that "Benbow blood will sort of
hold him down." After her husband's death she was courted
casually by various southern gentlemen, including Gowan
Stevens, but she showed more interest in the adventures of her
older brother, Horace Benbow. The recipient of eleven anonymous love letters (from Byron Snopes) during her courtship
by Bayard, Narcissa went to Memphis twelve years later and
slept with a Federal Agent in order to insure the final destruction of the letters. By so doing, she was deemed by Virginia Du
Pre a fitting guardian of the remnants of the Sartoris family.
Sartoris, Sanctuary, The Town, "There Was a Queen."

Saunders, Cecily. *See* Farr, Cecily Saunders.

Saunders, Minnie, wife of Robert Saunders and mother of Cecily
and Robert, Jr. Sharply aware of and obedient to the pressures
of her society, she taught her husband "better than to try to
drive a woman to do anything." *Soldiers' Pay.*

Saunders, Robert, a Charlestown, Georgia businessman. Husband
of Minnie, father of Cecily and Robert, Jr., "he was a Catholic,
which was almost as sinful as being a Republican," and a hard-
pressed family man, which was even more painful. *Soldiers' Pay.*

Saunders, Robert, Jr., the young son of Robert and Minnie Saunders. His greatest frustration occurred when he was not permitted to see the scar of returned war-hero Donald Mahon.
Soldiers' Pay.

Schluss, a salesman of ladies' underthings. This patriot, who had
"to look out for business while the boys are gone," became
entangled and intoxicated with Julian Lowe and Joe Gilligan
on the train heading west. *Soldiers' Pay.*

Schofield, Doctor, a Yoknapatawpha physician who amputated
Buddy McCallum's leg. "The Tall Men."

Schultz, Reverend, a protestant minister in Jefferson. He led the
efforts to "save" Uncle Willy Christian. "Uncle Willy."

Secretary, a "burr-headed" Negro boy who drove a car for Uncle
Willy Christian. "Uncle Willy."

Semitic Man. *See* Kauffman, Julius.

Semmes, a Memphis distiller. Boon Hogganbeck and Isaac Mc-
Caslin went all the way to Memphis to buy liquor from him
when they ran out at the de Spain hunting camp. "The Bear."

Sentry (**Mr. Harry, Mistairy**), a British private who joined the Northumberland Borderers in August, 1914. He was "a stupid, surly, dirty, unsocial, really unpleasant man." But during the war, this "inconsolable orphan" somehow compelled confidence and love, as evidenced by his being named beneficiary of insurance policies by a large share of his battalion. The men bet twenty shillings a month that they would be dead in thirty days; when they remained alive Sentry paid off; when they died he got the insurance. *A Fable.*

Short, Herman, a talented horse trader of Yoknapatawpha County. *The Hamlet.*

Shumann, Dr. Carl, father of Roger Shumann, "grandfather" of young Jack Shumann. He was a physician in Myron, Ohio. *Pylon.*

Shumann, Jack, the six-year-old son of Laverne Shumann and either Roger Shumann or Jack Holmes. He was born in California in a hangar on an old parachute. After Roger's death, the boy was taken to live with Shumann's parents in Ohio. *Pylon.*

Shumann, Laverne, the wife of Roger Shumann. An orphan, she was reared in Iowa but left the state during her high school days and spent the next years touring the country with two athletic fliers. After the birth of her son, Shumann and Jack Holmes rolled dice to decide which of them would marry her and give a name to the child. When Shumann died in the airplane crash, she was two months pregnant, but not with his child. *Pylon.*

Shumann, Roger, the son of Dr. Carl Shumann of Myron, Ohio. As a racing flier he toured the country with his wife Laverne and a parachute jumper, Jack Holmes. He was killed in the crash of a borrowed plane in New Valois (New Orleans), Louisiana. *Pylon.*

Sibbey. *See* McCaslin, Sophonsiba.

Simon. *See* Strother, Simon.

Skipworth, the Beat Four constable who handcuffed Lucas Beauchamp to a bedpost until Jefferson authorities arrived to take over this supposed murderer of Vinson Gowrie. *Intruder in the Dust.*

Smith, Essie Meadowfill (1925–   ), the daughter of miser Meadowfill. "A quiet modest mousy girl," she graduated in 1942 as valedictorian and took a job with the telephone company rather than accept a college scholarship because she wanted to earn enough money to put a bathroom in her home. Later she worked in the Jefferson bank until her marriage in 1946 to McKinley Smith, a marriage which was an "act of determination." *The Mansion.*

Smith, McKinley, an ex-Marine corporal, son of an east Texas tenant farmer. After two years in the service, he decided that "the only place you can be safe in is a private hole" and "I aim to own me a hole." He met Essie Meadowfill, "maybe through a lovelorn correspondence agency," and they were married in 1946. In building his new home in Eula Acres, he became involved in the running feud between old Meadowfill and Orestes Snopes. *The Mansion.*

Smith, Midshipman R. Boyce (Ronnie), the close-mouthed commander of a British torpedo ship during World War I. "Turnabout."

Snopes, Ab (Abner), progenitor of Snopesism in Yoknapatawpha County, father of Flem Snopes, Colonel Sartoris Snopes, and twin daughters, Net and Lizzie. He served as horse-thieving traitor in the Confederate Army, indiscriminate barn-burner, and accomplice in the murder of Rosa Millard. Uncle Buck McCaslin said that Colonel John Sartoris shot Ab for "trying to steal his clay-bank riding stallion during the war." *The Unvanquished, The Hamlet, The Town, The Mansion,* "Barn Burning," "My Grandmother Millard," "Vendée."

Snopes, Admiral Dewey, the son of Eck Snopes. He was six years younger than his brother, Wallstreet Panic. This family "had never been Snopeses to begin with." *The Hamlet, The Town, The Mansion.*

Snopes, Bilbo, one of the twin sons of I. O. Snopes by his second wife. *The Town, The Mansion.*

Snopes, Byron, a son of I. O. Snopes by his first wife. This one-time bookkeeper at the Sartoris bank looted the bank in the late 1920's and fled to El Paso, Texas. He sent back to Flem Snopes "C.O.D. four half-Snopes half-Apache Indian children," whom Clarence Snopes adopted and trained as a hunting pack until their behavior prompted Flem to return them to Texas. *Sartoris, The Town, The Mansion,* "The Waifs."

Snopes, Clarence Egglestone, the son of I. O. Snopes. A one-time constable of Frenchman's Bend, he "made the mistake of pistol-whipping in the name of the Law some feller that was spiteful and vindictive enough to resent being pistol-whipped." He advanced from constable to state senator and intended to run for Congress, until the "dog thicket" episode at the annual Varner's Mill picnic in 1945 dampened his desires and his trousers, thus allowing his really worthy opponent, Colonel Devries, to run unopposed. *Sanctuary, The Town, The Mansion,* "By the People," "The Waifs."

Snopes, Colonel Sartoris, a son of Ab Snopes. He ran away from home at the age of ten when he discovered that his father was a barn burner. *The Hamlet,* "Barn Burning."

Snopes, Doris, a son of I. O. Snopes, and the younger brother of Clarence Egglestone Snopes. He had the "mentality of a child" and the "moral principles of a wolverine." *The Town, The Mansion.*

Snopes, Eck (Eckrum), father of four children, including Wall-street Panic and Admiral Dewey. He worked at Will Varner's blacksmith shop and sawmill, in Flem Snopes's restaurant, and died executing his duties as night watchman at the railroad oil tank. He believed in the "incredible and innocent assumption that all people practice courage and honesty for the simple reason that if they didnt everybody would be frightened and confused." It was suspected that "Eck's mother took some extra-curricular night work nine months before he was born" and that consequently "the one technically true pristine immaculate unchallengeable son of a bitch" ever produced was not even a Snopes. *The Hamlet, The Town, The Mansion,* "Spotted Horses."

Snopes, Eula Varner (1889–1927), last of the sixteen children of influential businessman Will Varner. "Incorrigibly lazy" and not incorruptible, by age sixteen she was pregnant by Hoake McCarron. There followed a hastily arranged and paternally-financed marriage to Flem Snopes. For eighteen years she was the mistress of banker Manfred de Spain, her husband's principal social and business rival. During those years she remained Flem's wife only so that her daughter Linda could grow up not having to say "other children have got what I never had." When

Flem prepared to remove de Spain as bank president, Eula shot herself. *The Hamlet, The Town, The Mansion,* "Centaur in Brass."

Snopes, Flem (–1946), the son of Ab Snopes. This monumental figure "with eyes the color of stagnant water" arrived in Frenchman's Bend in the early 1900's wearing "that damn little ten-cent snap-on bow tie" and a "cloth cap about the size for a fourteen-year-old child." As a clerk in Will Varner's store, he learned about money: "that the only limit to the amount of money you could shut your hands on and keep and hold was just how much money there was. . . ." As the only man in Frenchman's Bend "that ever stood up to and held his own with old Will Varner," he married Eula Varner "to save her from dropping a bastard" and for a free deed to the Old Frenchman Place. By devious means and cool, unflagging hard work, he moved from clerk to restraurant owner and manager, to superintendent of the municipal power plant, to (by 1916) vice president of the Sartoris Bank, to president of the Merchants and Farmers Bank by 1924. What Flem wanted above all, according to V. K. Ratliff, one of his foremost opponents, was respectability. Impotent, he set out to prove the validity of the claim that "there ain't a man in Missippi nor the U.S. and A. put together that can beat Flem Snopes." That statement held until the release from prison in 1946 of one of his numerous kinsmen, Mink Snopes. Bent on revenge, Mink fulfilled a thirty-eight-year-old dream: the shooting and death of Flem, while his victim sat immobile, detached, waiting for the end. *Sartoris, As I Lay Dying, The Hamlet, The Town, The Mansion, The Reivers,* "Centaur in Brass," "Spotted Horses," "The Hound," "Lizards in Jamshyd's Courtyard," "The Waifs."

Snopes, I. O., a first cousin of Flem Snopes. Typical of his incapacity for doing anything straightforwardly was his marital entanglement. A bigamist, by "wife no. 1" he had two sons, Byron and Virgil; by "wife no. 2" he had six sons, Clarence, Doris, twins Bilbo and Vardaman, Montgomery Ward, and Saint Elmo. Inherently crooked, and guided by cousin Flem, he served the area variously as blacksmith, schoolteacher, restaurant manager and hotel proprietor. His most spectacular venture was a partnership with Lonzo Hait in which they purchased mules in Memphis, tied them to the railroad track, and collected insurance from the railroad, even on the rope. By 1920 Flem, concerned about his own respectability, had had enough and "ci-devanted I. O. back to Frenchman's Bend for good." *The Sound and the Fury, The Hamlet, The Town, The Mansion,* "Mule in the Yard."

Snopes, Ike (Isaac), a drooling idiot. Unlike other members of the Snopes tribe, Ike was in love, not with money, position, or women, but with a cow. *The Hamlet.*

Snopes, Linda. *See* Kohl, Linda Snopes.

Snopes, Lizzie, daughter of Ab Snopes, twin of Net. *The Unvanquished.*

Snopes, Lump (Launcelot), a cousin of Flem Snopes. His mother was a schoolteacher who believed "that there was honor and pride and salvation and hope too to be found for man's example between the pages of books"; his father was at one time "under indictment . . . because of a drummer's sample-case of shoes, all for the right foot, which had vanished from a railway baggage-room." In typical Snopes fashion he succeeded Flem as clerk in Will Varner's store when Flem married Eula Varner. One of his sordid enterprises was the exploitation of his relative, Ike Snopes. *The Hamlet, The Mansion.*

Snopes, Mink (1883–   ), married in 1903, the father of two children. He was sent to prison in 1908 for the murder of Jack Houston, resulting from his refusal to pay Houston "that ere extry one-dollar pound fee" for pasturage of a cow. Twenty more years were added to his sentence when his escape from prison was foiled, thanks to the family efforts of Flem and Montgomery Ward Snopes. Due to be released in 1948, he was freed in 1946 on the basis of a petition by Linda Snopes Kohl, and after an almost epic struggle, this "only out-and-out mean Snopes" achieved his heartfelt and long-awaited revenge: the killing of cousin Flem Snopes. *See* Cotton, Ernest. *The Hamlet, The Town, The Mansion.*

Snopes, Montgomery Ward, the son of I. O. Snopes by his second "wife," and a second cousin to Flem Snopes. Refused enlistment by the army during World War I because of a heart condition, he learned much by serving the YMCA in France. On his return to Yoknapatawpha County, he opened the "Atelier Monty," a highly profitable shop dealing in filthy pictures. As a result, in 1923 he was sent to Parchman prison, although the charge was for selling moonshine. This change of indictment was credited to cousin Flem Snopes, who preferred Monty in Parchman rather than in a federal prison so that he might trick Mink Snopes into trying to escape, a ruse which succeeded. After his own release from prison, Montgomery Ward departed from Flem's realm and was last heard of in Los Angeles, involved with "some quite lucrative adjunct or correlative" to the motion picture industry. *Sartoris, The Town, The Mansion.*

Snopes, Net, daughter of Ab Snopes, twin of Lizzie. *The Unvanquished,* "Barn Burning."

Snopes, Orestes, another member of the Snopes tribe. He appeared in Jefferson after World War II and began acting as Flem Snopes's land agent in transforming the old Compson property into building lots for a veteran's housing project to be known as Eula Acres. In so doing he carried on a kind of classic "guerrilla feud" with miserly neighbor Meadowfill. *The Mansion.*

Snopes, Saint Elmo, youngest son of I. O. Snopes. A hulking boy, with a "vast, flaccid colorless face," he had a voracious appetite, and according to Will Varner would "work through that lace leather and them hame-strings and lap-links and ring-bolts and eat me and you. . . ." *The Hamlet.*

Snopes, Vardaman, one of the twin sons of I. O. Snopes by his second wife. *The Town, The Mansion.*

Snopes, Virgil, the son of I. O. Snopes (according to *The Town*); the son of Wesley Snopes (according to *The Mansion*). When he and Fonzo Winbush (two "innocents") arrived in Memphis to attend barber's college, they rented a room in Reba Rivers' house, thinking it a rooming house. Under the tutelage and sponsorship of his cousin, Clarence Snopes, Virgil proved to be "a really exceptional talent" at satisfying two girls in succession. *Sanctuary, The Town, The Mansion.*

Snopes, Vynie, the first wife of Ab Snopes. *The Hamlet,* "Fool About a Horse."

Snopes, Wallstreet Panic, the non-Snopes son of a non-Snopes,

Eck. Wallstreet did not start kindergarten until he was twelve years old, but he graduated from high school at age sixteen. Through simple honesty and industry, he became owner of his own store when he was nineteen, resisted Flem Snopes's efforts to ruin him, established the first self-service grocery store in Jefferson, and soon owned a chain of them in northern Mississippi. He married a woman who did not want to change the Snopeses; she just wanted to live them down. They moved from Jefferson to Memphis. *The Hamlet, The Town, The Mansion,* "Spotted Horses."

Snopes, Watkins Products, a carpenter in Jefferson. One of the Snopeses "who could read reading," he was hired by Flem Snopes to "transform the old de Spain house into Flem's antebellum mansion." *The Mansion.*

Snopes, Wesley, an uncle of the children of I. O. Snopes. He was capable of "leading a hymn with one hand and fumbling the skirt of an eleven-year-old infant with the other." *The Mansion.*

Sometimes-Wakeup, the brother of old Issetibbeha. After the deaths of his brother and his brother's son, Moketubbe, he said he did not want to be "The Man." "A Justice."

Son Thomas, the youngest driver for Maury Priest's livery stable in Jefferson. *The Reivers.*

Sophonsiba. *See* McCaslin, Sophonsiba (Sibbey).

Sophonsiba (Fonsiba) (1869–   ), the fifth child of Tennie Beauchamp and Tomey's Turl. In 1886 she married a northern Negro who had been granted a farm in Arkansas by the federal government in recognition of his military service. After her marriage she was not seen again. "The Bear."

Spoade, a Harvard senior from South Carolina. A friend of Quentin Compson, he was "the world's champion sitter-around." *The Sound and the Fury.*

Spoomer, a captain in the British air force, and a friend of the Sartoris twins. "All the Dead Pilots."

Spratling, William, the name of an actual person. He was an artist and friend of William Faulkner. "Out of Nazareth," "Episode."

Stamper, Pat, a sharp horse trader. In the horse and mule circles of a large section of the South he was to other traders "what Fritz Kreisler would be to the fiddle player at a country picnic," and yet he only "broke even" with Flem Snopes. *The Hamlet, The Mansion,* "Fool About a Horse."

Starnes, a hill-country farmer. He was murdered by his wife's lover. "The Liar."

Starnes, a family to whom Henry (Hawkshaw) Stribling felt an obligation. After struggling for thirteen years he paid off a debt of theirs. "Hair."

Steinbauer, Genevieve (Jenny), a vague pretty blonde who received a last-minute casual invitation from Pat Robyn to join the Maurier yachting party. With Pete Ginotta she did so, and was kept alert repelling the advances of most of the men on board. *Mosquitoes.*

Stevens, Mrs., the wife of Judge Lemuel Stevens, mother of twins, Margaret Stevens Mallison and Gavin Stevens. She "wouldn't abide tea; she said it was for sick people." "Knight's Gambit."

Stevens, Bucky, the young son of Gowan and Temple Drake Stevens. *Requiem for a Nun.*

Stevens, Gavin (1889–   ), the son of Judge Lemuel Stevens, "born into a gossamer-sinewed envelope of boundless and hopeless aspiration." A Phi Beta Kappa graduate of the state university, he earned an M.A. at Harvard and a Ph.D. at Heidelberg. In 1916–17 he served abroad in the American Field Service. Upon return to Jefferson he acted as private defender, county attorney, lawyer, and judge. Besides the law, his principal interests were the Snopeses—he considered Flem Snopes "his mortal victorious rival and conqueror"—Eula Varner Snopes, her daughter, Linda Snopes Kohl, and society in general. His sister, Margaret Mallison, his nephew, Chick Mallison, and his friend, V. K. Ratliff, found him a source of confidence, hope, and countywide information. In 1942 he married Melisandre Backus Harriss, daughter of old Jefferson stock. Of himself he said, "I am happy I was given the privilege of meddling with impunity in other people's affairs without really doing any harm by belonging to that avocation whose acolytes have been absolved in advance for holding justice above truth." *Light in August, Intruder in the Dust, Requiem for a Nun, The Town, The Mansion,* "Go Down, Moses," "Knight's Gambit," "Smoke," "Monk," "Hand Upon the Waters," "Tomorrow," "An Error in Chemistry," "Hair," "By the People," "The Waifs."

Stevens, Gowan, a cousin of Chick Mallison, and "nephew" of Gavin Stevens. His grandfather was a brother of Chick's grandfather. Gowan was "almost a type": the son of financially secure parents—his father worked for the State Department; an alumnus of a good college—the University of Virginia, where he learned to drink like a gentleman. After proposing marriage to Narcissa Benbow Sartoris, who refused him, he embarked on a critical weekend drinking spree with Temple Drake. In a drunken stupor he deserted her, leaving her to Popeye Vitelli, and spent the rest of his days seeking his former status. He and Temple were married in Paris at the embassy the winter following her return to her family from the Memphis house of prostitution. Then they went back to Jefferson, where two children, a son and daughter, were born to them. Only after the murder of their baby daughter by their Negro servant, Nancy Mannigoe, and the ensuing confessions of Temple, was Gowan able to see peace ahead for himself and his wife. *Sanctuary, Requiem for a Nun, The Town.*

Stevens, Judge Lemuel (–1918), the father of twins, Gavin and Margaret Stevens Mallison. As mayor of Jefferson he was asked to do something about the smell coming from Miss Emily Grierson's house. He replied, "Dammit, sir, will you accuse a lady to her face of smelling bad?" *The Town, The Mansion, The Reivers,* "A Rose for Emily."

Stevens, Melisandre Backus Harriss, the wife of Gavin Stevens. A daughter of old Jefferson stock and a graduate of the Female Academy, she preceded Linda Snopes as a protégé of Stevens, but when he returned from the war she "had committed the irrevocable error" of growing up and marrying Harriss, a New Orleans "underworld big shot," by whom she had a son and a daughter. After Harriss' murder, she and her children and five servants traveled and lived abroad. In 1942 she married Stevens. *The Mansion,* "Knight's Gambit."

Stevens, Temple Drake, the only daughter of Judge Drake of Jackson. She and her four brothers came from a highly respected family. By the age of eighteen, this flapper, accused of being the sort who will "take all you can get and give nothing," had disgraced herself and her family, been brutally raped, and was residing in a Memphis house of prostitution. There she fell in love with Alabama Red, the stud who had been supplied by her psychopathic abductor Popeye Vitelli. Her marriage at the Paris embassy to Gowan Stevens, the blackmail plot of Red's brother Pete, and the murder of her six-month-old daughter by "reformed whore" Nancy Mannigoe, eventually convinced her that one must face the truth or pay for the past. *Sanctuary*, *Requiem for a Nun*.

Stokes, the manager of the Compson farm. "A Justice."

Stone, an Oxford lawyer. He had attended Yale and drew up Linda Snopes Kohl's will, in which she bequeathed everything to Flem Snopes. *The Town*.

Stovall, a Jefferson bank cashier and Baptist deacon. He frequented the pleasures of Nancy, a Negro laundress who worked for the Compsons, but when she asked for payment he kicked her teeth in. "That Evening Sun."

Stribling, Henry (Hawkshaw), a Jefferson barber. He gave Susan Reed her first haircut, and later married her. "Hair," "Dry September."

Stribling, Susan Reed, a Jefferson orphan. She married Henry Stribling. "Hair."

Strother, Caspey, a Negro servant of the Sartoris family. He was the brother of Elnora (according to *Sartoris*); he was the husband of Elnora (according to "There Was a Queen"). He served in France during World War I, and served time in the penitentiary for stealing. *Sartoris*, "There Was a Queen."

Strother, Elnora, the daughter of Colonel John Sartoris. She was married to Caspey and bore three children, Joby, Saddie, and Isom. (According to *Sartoris*, she was the sister of Caspey.) She devoted her life to faithful service of the Sartoris family. *Sartoris*, "There Was a Queen."

Strother, Isom (1903–   ), the son of Elnora Strother. *Sartoris*, "There Was a Queen."

Strother, Simon, the Negro husband of Elnora Strother's mother. The grandson of Joby and Louvinia, he served the Sartoris family all of his life. He was found murdered at the Meloney Harris place. *Sartoris*, "There Was a Queen."

Strutterbuck, Captain, a Memphis resident. "Tall, pretty big, with a kind of roustabout's face," this braggart was an irregular visitor at Reba Rivers' house, where his prowess as a man and as soldier of two wars were both readily disproved. *The Mansion.*

Studenmare, Captain, a Mississippi River steamboat owner. "A Courtship."

Suratt, V. K. *See* Ratliff.

Sutpen, Clytemnestra (1834—December, 1909, according to *Absalom, Absalom!*; 1910, according to "Genealogy"). Born at Sutpen's Hundred, "Clytie" was the daughter of Thomas Sutpen and a Negro slave. She represented "in the very pigmentation of her flesh . . . that debacle" which had made southerners what they were. "Free, yet incapable of freedom who had never once called herself a slave," she was at once loyal to and independent of her Sutpen charges: caring for the idiot Jim Bond for twenty-six years; hiding and protecting Henry Sutpen for four years; and dying with him in the fire which destroyed the mansion. This "tiny gnomelike creature" remained an inscrutable paradox: "half untamed black, half Sutpen." *Absalom, Absalom!*

Sutpen, Ellen Coldfield (1818, according to "Genealogy"; October 9, 1817, according to *Absalom, Absalom!*—1862, according to "Genealogy"; January 23, 1863, according to *Absalom, Absalom!*), the Tennessee-born daughter of Goodhue Coldfield, and second wife of Thomas Sutpen in 1838, a marriage "she washed out of her remembering with tears," and mother of Henry and Judith. Placing her "outrageous husband and incomprehensible children" in limbo, this "butterfly" escaped "into a world of pure illusion" until, caused by no specifically stated ailment, she entered "dissolution by actually dissolving," entrusting the care of her twenty-one-year-old daughter to her seventeen-year-old sister, Rosa Coldfield. *Absalom, Absalom!*

Sutpen, Eulalia, born and reared in Haiti, the daughter of a wealthy French sugar plantation owner. She married her father's overseer, Thomas Sutpen, in 1827. A son, Charles Bon, was born to them, but was never acknowledged by his father. After being "put aside" by Sutpen, who doubted the purity of her blood, she devoted her energies to preparing her son to claim his heritage. No specific statement is made concerning a divorce from Sutpen. Her death occurred in New Orleans. *Absalom, Absalom!*

Sutpen, Henry (1839—December, 1909, according to *Absalom,*

Absalom!; 1910, according to "Genealogy"), the Mississippi-born son of Thomas and Ellen Coldfield Sutpen. He attended the University of Mississippi, meeting there his fate, in Charles Bon, and with him served in the University Greys during the war; Henry was wounded at Shiloh. Even at age sixteen he gave "promise of someday standing eye to eye with his father." The time came when "he gave his father the lie," and out of love or loyalty to Bon he repudiated birthplace and heritage, only later, in 1865, to be forced by that heritage to destroy the brotherhood because of the threat of miscegenation, not because of incest. Decades of wandering, culminating in four years of isolated horror in the rotting Sutpen mansion, ended in fire and his death. *Absalom, Absalom!*

Sutpen, Judith (1841–84), the Mississippi-born daughter of Thomas and Ellen Coldfield Sutpen, sister of Henry. A dreamer, she lived in almost "complete detachment and imperviousness to actuality." Engaged largely through the efforts of her mother to Charles Bon, she waited for the war's end, serving as "the blank shape, the empty vessel" in which Bon and her brother Henry each "strove to preserve . . . his illusion of the other." Just as patiently, in 1865, she stood by as her brother murdered her fiancé, and then calmly suggested that all move downstairs so that she could order some planks and nails for the coffin. Seven months later she burst into tears when reporting the event to her father on his return from the war. She died (from yellow fever, according to *Absalom, Absalom!*; from smallpox, according to the "Chronology") after a vain attempt to save Bon's bastard son, Charles Etienne Bon, from the disease. *Absalom, Absalom!*

Sutpen, Thomas (1807—August 12, 1869), the West Virginia-born son of a Tidewater drunkard and a mountain woman who never learned to speak English. At age fourteen he learned that there were differences between men and concluded that to combat the rich "you have got to have what they have that made them do what the man did." The rest of his days were devoted to the furtherance of that creed, to the building of a dynasty. With that aim, he went to sea in 1823. He married first Eulalia, the daughter of a planter, only to decide later that "she would not be adjunctive or incremental" to his design; in 1838 he married Ellen Coldfield and by her had two children, Henry and Judith, who destroyed themselves and his third unacknowledged child, Charles Bon. After serving well during the war as a colonel, he returned to reclaim his property, and to further his single-minded desire to have a son to inherit the land; for this reason he turned to sixteen-year-old Milly Jones, and because of this he was killed by Wash Jones, leaving as his sole survivor "one Nigger Sutpen," Jim Bond. *Absalom, Absalom!, The Unvanquished, Requiem for a Nun,* "The Bear," "Wash," "The Old People."

Sutterfield, Tobe (Monsieur Tooleyman), a Negro minister whose pseudonym was derived from his position with the Association of Les Amis Myriades et Anonymes à la France de Tout le Monde. He and his twelve-year-old grandson traveled with the remarkable horse and the Sentry, sharing "a bond stronger than even the golden shackles." According to him, "God dont need me. I bears witness to Him of course, but my main witness is to man." His aim was to show that "all you can kill is man's meat. You cant kill his voice." *A Fable.*

Sylvester's John, a young Indian. "A Courtship."

T

T. P., the son of Dilsey. He drove for the Compsons, and helped take care of Benjy Compson. *The Sound and the Fury,* "That Evening Sun."

Talliaferro (Tarver), Ernest, a thirty-eight-year-old widower, originally from Alabama. A wholesale buyer of women's clothes in New Orleans, he had had "careful raising" and "had been forced while quite young and pliable to do all the things to which his natural impulses objected, and to forego all the things he could possibly have had any fun doing." His trouble, by middle age, was "the illusion that you can seduce women." *Mosquitoes.*

Tennie's Jim. *See* Beauchamp, James.

Terrel, Bill, a prison inmate serving a twenty-year sentence for manslaughter. He tricked Monk Odlethrop into murdering the warden. "Monk."

Theule, the "fat one" among the "pint-sized dark men" in the bayous who daily watched the Tall Convict in combat with the alligators. *The Wild Palms.*

Thompson, "Pappy," grandfather of Roz. He was attacked by Joe Christmas in the Negro church. *Light in August.*

Thompson, Roz, a Negro who tried to defend his grandfather, "Pappy" Thompson, against the maniacal attack in the Negro church by Joe Christmas. Roz was found later with a fractured skull caused by a single savage blow dealt by Christmas. *Light in August.*

Thorpe, Buck, the illegitimate son of a woman who died giving birth to him. He was unofficially adopted by the woman's husband, Stonewall Jackson Fentry, who named the boy Jackson and Longstreet Fentry. He was soon taken by his mother's brothers and reared to become "a swaggering bravo" of Frenchman's Bend. His occupations included gambling, brawling, the distillation of illegal whiskey, and cattle theft. The attempt to elope with Odum Bookwright's daughter resulted in his murder by Bookwright. "Tomorrow."

Thucydus. *See* Roskus, Thucydus.

Tobe, the loyal, quiet old Negro servant of Emily Grierson. "A Rose for Emily."

Tom Tom Bird, one of the firemen at the Jefferson power plant. *The Town,* "Centaur in Brass."

Tomasina (Tomy, Tomey) (1810—June, 1833), daughter of Lucius Q. C. McCaslin and Eunice Roskus, a house servant who held herself "something above the other slaves." Tomasina died in childbirth, leaving a son, Turl (Terrel), sired by Lucius Q. C. McCaslin. "The Bear."

Tomey's Turl (Terrel) (June, 1833–   ), the son of Lucius Quintus Carothers McCaslin and Tomasina. Every time he could slip off from Uncle Buck and Uncle Buddy McCaslin's place he would hang around Hubert Beauchamp's girl, Tennie. Finally, in 1859, after Uncle Buddy won her in a poker game with Beauchamp, Tennie and Tomey's Turl were married. They were the parents of six children, the last three of whom were

James Thucydus Beauchamp (Tennie's Jim), Sophonsiba (Fonsiba), and Lucas Beauchamp. Decades later, Tomey's Turl was hired to fire the boilers at the Jefferson power plant under superintendent Flem Snopes. *The Town*, "The Bear," "Was," "The Fire and the Hearth," "Delta Autumn," "Centaur in Brass."

Tommy (Tawmmy), the kind-hearted "feeb," a member of the Lee Goodwin bootlegging organization near Jefferson. Although he had been seen and known around the countryside for fifteen years, no one knew the last name of this "barefoot, hatless" innocent with "his rapt, empty gaze." He was murdered June 17, 1929, by Popeye Vitelli. *Sanctuary*.

Tony the Wop, a friend of Jean-Baptiste. "Home."

Tooleyman. *See* Sutterfield, Tobe.

Top, the son of Big Top and Guster. He was a childhood companion to Gowan Stevens. *The Town*.

Triplett, Earl, a delta resident brought to Jefferson by Isaac McCaslin to run his hardware store. Triplett "gently eliminated" Ike from the store, and in turn was himself later eliminated from it by Jason Compson. *The Sound and the Fury, The Mansion*.

Trueblood, Ernest V. (Ernest be Toogood), the pseudonym under which Faulkner wrote the story "Afternoon of a Cow." Trueblood narrates the tale. "Afternoon of a Cow."

Trumbull, the Frenchman's Bend blacksmith for almost twenty years. He was succeeded by Eck Snopes. *The Hamlet, The Town*.

Tubbs, Euphus, the Jefferson jailer. Because of their occupation, he and his wife knew a large number of Yoknapatawpha residents. One of Mrs. Tubbs's more thoughtful acts was to hang an old shade over the cell window so that the morning sun would not wake Montgomery Ward Snopes. *Intruder in the Dust, Requiem for a Nun, The Mansion*.

Tucker, Mr. and Mrs., Mottstown residents and victims of Rodney who planned to run away with Mrs. Tucker. "That Will be Fine."

Tull, Cora, the wife of Vernon Tull. Originally from Alabama, this one-time schoolteacher was a "do-gooder." Of her Addie Bundren said that she was "one of those people to whom sin is just a matter of words, to them salvation is just words too." Indicative of Cora's effect on people were her husband's words that "if nothing but being married will help a man, he's durn nigh hopeless." *As I Lay Dying, The Hamlet, The Town, The Mansion.*

Tull, Odum, a resident of Frenchman's Bend. "Fool About a Horse."

Tull, Vernon, a fairly well-to-do farmer of Frenchman's Bend. Married to Cora, and the father of four daughters, he had "the face of the breathing archetype and protagonist of all men who marry young and father only daughters and are themselves but the eldest daughter of their own wives." He proved to be a good neighbor to the Bundren family, although he wondered whether they were worth the effort. *As I Lay Dying, Sanctuary, The Hamlet, The Town, The Mansion,* "Shingles for the Lord," "The Hound," "Lizards in Jamshyd's Courtyard."

Turpin, one of the "timorous local stallions" of Frenchman's Bend who tried desperately and hopelessly to ravish Eula Varner. *The Hamlet, The Mansion.*

U

Uncle Ash. *See* Wylie, Uncle Ash.
Uncle Buck. *See* McCaslin, Theophilus.
Uncle Buddy. *See* McCaslin, Amodeus.
Uncle Ike. *See* McCaslin, Isaac.
Uncle Possum. *See* Hood, Parsham.
Uncle Willy. *See* Christian, Uncle Willy.

V

Van, one of the hired help at Lee Goodwin's bootlegging head-quarters near Jefferson. Goodwin was forced to knock him out to keep him from "pestering" Temple Drake. *Sanctuary.*

Van Dyming, Mrs. Mathilda Lumpkin, a wealthy Park Avenue society matron. "Black Music."

Van Tosch, the owner of Lightning (Coppermine), the "stolen" horse ridden in the historic Parsham Races by Lucius Priest. *The Reivers*.

Vardaman. *See* Bundren, Vardaman.

Varner, Eula. *See* Snopes, Eula Varner.

Varner, Jody (1888–   ), the "oafish troglodyte son" of Will Varner. A bachelor, the ninth of sixteen children, he managed his father's store in Frenchman's Bend and acted as overseer for some of his scattered farms. *As I Lay Dying, The Hamlet, The Town, The Mansion*, "Fool About a Horse," "Spotted Horses."

Varner, Will, the "chief man" of the Frenchman's Bend district. Farmer, politician, storekeeper, veterinarian, Methodist lay preacher, usurer, justice of the peace—before he was forty he "had shaved notes and foreclosed liens and padded furnish bills and evicted tenants until the way Will Varner went Frenchman's Bend had done already left." Married twice, he was the father of sixteen children by his first wife; he married the second time a girl of twenty-five, after he had been widowed for over ten years and was in his early eighties. Judge Benbow once said of him that "a milder-mannered man never bled a mule or stuffed a ballot box." *See* Gibson, Will. *As I Lay Dying, Light in August, The Hamlet, The Town, The Mansion*, "Spotted Horses," "Shingles for the Lord," "Tomorrow," "Lizards in Jamshyd's Courtyard," "By the People."

Varner, Mrs. Will, the mother of sixteen children. A "big hard cold gray woman," she divided her time between her home and her church. *The Hamlet, The Town*.

Vatch, the older brother of a Tennessee family. He served with the Union Army during the Civil War and was responsible for the deaths of Major Saucier Weddel and of his own brother, Hule. "Mountain Victory."

Venturia, Juan, a French Quarter resident. His greatest delight was in harassing his neighbor Harris. "The Rosary."

Versh, the son of Dilsey. *The Sound and the Fury*, "That Evening Sun."

Vines, Deacon, the Negro leader of the church near Jefferson. He sent for police help during the savage onslaught in the church by Joe Christmas. *Light in August*.

Vinson, Mrs., the proprietor of a Mississippi country inn. She went off to Memphis with Jim Gant and was murdered there by Jim's wife. *Miss Zilphia Gant.*

Vitelli, Popeye, a psychopath, sadist, and murderer. Born on Christmas Day, the son of a department store clerk and a professional strike-breaker, he was blighted from birth because of the "legacy" of venereal disease left his mother by "her brief husband." He did not learn to walk or talk until he was nearly four years old, had no hair until he was five, had such a delicate digestive system that convulsions resulted from the slightest deviation from a strict regime, and "properly speaking" he "would never be a man." After five years in an institution for incorrigible children, he left home, returning to Pensacola each summer to visit his mother, who believed that he was a night clerk in a Memphis hotel. "Prosperous, quiet, thin, black, and uncommunicative . . . he had that vicious depthless quality of stamped tin." Known by no one and feared by nearly everyone in his bootlegging underworld, he proved a fascination to Temple Drake, whom he had brutally assaulted and then removed to a Memphis house of prostitution. The murderer of Tommy and of Alabama Red, he was arrested, convicted, and hanged for a murder he did not commit. His last words were, "Fix my hair, Jack." *Sanctuary, Requiem for a Nun.*

W

Waldrip, Mrs. Vernon, the faithless sweetheart of the Tall Convict. *The Wild Palms.*

Walkley, a British officer during World War I, hospitalized with Alexander Gray. After the armistice he emigrated from England to Canada, where he became a wheat farmer. "Victory."

Waller, Hamp, a countryman of Yoknapatawpha County. He and his wife discovered the fire and the mutilated corpse of Joanna Burden in the burning house. *Light in August.*

Warden, the man in charge of Parchman prison to which Mink Snopes was sent. After becoming somewhat acquainted with the Snopes myth, he wished that he "didn't know as much already as I suspect." *The Mansion.*

Wardle, Mrs., a Charlestown, Georgia, social arbiter. *Soldiers' Pay.*

Warren, Captain, a farmer who lived a few miles from Jefferson. He had been a flight commander in the Royal Flying Corps in World War I. "Knight's Gambit," "Death Drag."

Wash. *See* Jones, Wash.

Wattman, Jakeleg, one of the many bootleggers in Yoknapatawpha County. He ran a "so-called fishing camp" at Wyatt's Crossing, and among his customers was Linda Snopes Kohl. *The Mansion.*

Weddel, Francis, the son of Francois Vidal, a New Orleans Frenchman, and of a Choctaw squaw; the father of Saucier Weddel. As chief of the Chickasaw nation he personally represented his people to President Jackson over a question of the possession of a river ford. "Lo!"

Weddel, Grenier, a bachelor, the kind Gavin Stevens said "would still be one no matter how many times who married him." *The Town.*

Weddel, Major Saucier (1837–65), the son of Francis Weddel, a Choctaw chief. He lost his arm fighting for the Confederates. After the war, en route to his home, "Contalmaison," in Mississippi, he was killed by a shell-shocked Union Army veteran, Vatch, in Tennessee. "Mountain Victory."

West, Doctor, a Jefferson drugstore owner. "Smoke."

West, David, a tramp-wanderer originally from Indiana, and a temporary steward on the Maurier yacht. He ran off briefly with Pat Robyn, but their idyllic interlude was harshly shattered by an onslaught of mosquitoes. *Mosquitoes.*

White, Caroline. *See* Sartoris, Caroline White.

Whitely, an RAF officer in World War I. "Thrift."

Whitfield, Reverend, the preacher at Frenchman's Bend and father of Jewel Bundren. His conscience bothered him mildly until he learned that Addie Bundren, Jewel's mother, was dying. He "wrestled with Satan" and "emerged victorious" convinced that God would "accept the will for the deed." *As I Lay Dying, The Hamlet,* "Shingles for the Lord," "Tomorrow."

Wid(d)rington, Mrs., the wife of the Standard Oil Company manager in Rincon, Mexico. "Carcassonne," "Black Music."

Widrington, Mrs., the childless owner of a $500 Pekinese which disappeared mysteriously in the vicinity of the cave where Byron Snopes's four Indian-Snopes children lived. *The Town,* "The Waifs."

Wilbourne, Henry (Harry) (1910–   ), the son of a doctor. He trained to be a doctor and was interning in a New Orleans hospital when he met Charlotte Rittenmeyer, wife of Francis Rittenmeyer and mother of two girls. Charlotte and Harry abandoned home and profession to "be together and eat together and sleep together." When, later, Charlotte's pregnancy threatened to disrupt this pattern, he reluctantly agreed to attempt an abortion. The operation failed, she died, and he was sentenced to the penitentiary. *The Wild Palms.*

Wilkins, a university professor in whose home Bayard Sartoris lived while attending the state university. *The Unvanquished.*

Wilkins, George (1916–   ), the husband of Nat Beauchamp Wilkins, and son-in-law of Lucas Beauchamp. This "jimber-jawed clown" for a brief time ran a still in competition with his father-in-law, and later joined him in operating a divining machine in a search for buried money. "The Fire and the Hearth," "Gold Is Not Always," "A Point of Law."

Wilkins, Nat Beauchamp (1923–   ), the daughter of Lucas Beauchamp, the last and youngest of his children, and wife of George Wilkins. *Intruder in the Dust,* "The Fire and the Hearth," "A Point of Law."

Wilmoth, editor of the Jefferson newspaper. He reluctantly but graciously agreed not to print the news concerning the crime and execution of Samuel Worsham Beauchamp, only to learn later that the boy's grandmother had wanted everything printed. "Go Down, Moses."

Winbush, Fonzo, a nephew of Grover Winbush. In his "simple Yoknapatawpha juvenile rural innocence" he and Virgil Snopes rented a room at Reba Rivers' house of prostitution while they attended barber's college in Memphis. *Sanctuary, The Mansion.*

Winbush, Grover, a one-time part owner with V. K. Ratliff of a Jefferson cafe. As night marshal he innocently helped wreck the dirty postcard business of Montgomery Ward Snopes when he was caught slipping out of the alley near the store. *The Town, The Mansion.*

Winterbottom, a Frenchman's Bend resident, proprietor of the boarding house where Launcelot Snopes lived. *Light in August, The Hamlet,* "Spotted Horses."

Wiseman, Eva, the sister of Julius Kauffman, and member of the "artistic" Maurier yachting party. *Mosquitoes.*

Woman, The, a pregnant flood victim whom the Tall Convict was sent to rescue. Serene, confident, and competent, she delivered her own child on the river bank and accompanied the Tall Convict as he endeavored to fulfill his mission. *The Wild Palms.*

Wop, The, a New Orleans thug who killed Johnny Gray after a street fight. "The Kid Learns."

Workitt, Sudley, an old man who had an agreement to sell timber to Vinson and Crawford Gowrie, and was being swindled by the latter. The discovery of this fact led to murder. *Intruder in the Dust.*

Workman, a Yoknapatawpha County insurance adjuster. "An Error in Chemistry."

Worsham, Dr., a Jefferson minister who was supposed to bury Rosa Millard. *The Unvanquished,* "The Unvanquished."

Worsham, Belle, an aging spinster whose home was on the outskirts of Jefferson. She lived alone, except for Hamp Worsham, a descendant of one of her father's slaves, and Hamp's wife. "Go Down, Moses."

Worsham, Hamp, the brother of Molly Worsham Beauchamp. He and his wife were the old servants of aging Miss Worsham. "Go Down, Moses."

Worthington, Mrs., a Charlestown, Georgia widow who "suffered from gout and a flouted will." A social leader of the town, "she believed in rights for women, as long as women would let her dictate what was right for them." *Soldiers' Pay.*

Wright, Doc, a Jefferson citizen who hung around the telegraph office, interested in tips on the stock market. *The Sound and the Fury.*

Wyatt, George, a Jefferson businessman and long-time friend of Colonel John Sartoris. He supported the Colonel and Drusilla Hawk during the election, and offered "to take off your hands" Bayard's revenge for the murder of his father. *The Unvanquished.*

Wyatt, Henry, a member of the annual hunting party which included Carothers Edmonds and nearly eighty-year-old Isaac McCaslin. "Delta Autumn."

Wyatt, Aunt Sally, a neighbor of the Benbow family, and companion to Narcissa Benbow during World War I. *Sartoris*.

Wylie, Job, a Negro assistant for Uncle Willy Christian. "Uncle Willy."

Wylie, Old Man Ash, the son of Uncle Ash Wylie. He succeeded his father as de Spain's camp cook and helper. "A Bear Hunt."

Wylie, Uncle Ash, the father of Old Man Ash Wylie. He was "by profession a camp cook and . . . did little else save cook for Major de Spain's hunting and camping parties." "The Old People," "The Bear," "A Bear Hunt."

Wyott, Dr., the President Emeritus of the Academy in Jefferson. *The Town*.

Wyott, Vaiden, a Jefferson second grade teacher. She tutored Wallstreet Panic Snopes, and was proposed to by him when he graduated from high school. She turned him down and shortly afterwards accepted a teaching position in Bristol, Virginia. *The Town*.

Y

Yo Ho, a Chinese mess boy on the British ship "Diana." He was accidentally killed by Freddie Ayers. "Yo Ho and Two Bottles of Rum."

Z

Zilich, Mrs. Sophie, a New York neighbor of Mrs. Margaret Noonan Gihon. "Pennsylvania Station."

Zsettlani, Piotr (Pierre Bouc), a Middle Easterner among the Corporal's group who denied his name and his leader. *A Fable*.

COMPSON

Quentin MacLachan Compson
(1699–1783)
|
Charles Stuart Compson
|
Jason Lycurgus Compson
|
Quentin MacLachan Compson
(the Old Governor)
|
Gen. Jason Lycurgus Compson, II
(–1900)
|
Jason Richmond Lycurgus Compson, III····Carolyn Bascomb

? ⌇Candace····Sydney Head   Jason, IV
(1892–   )   (1894–   )

Quentin   Maury/Benjamin
(1911–   )   (April 7, 1895–
                                   ca. 1936, acc. to
Quentin, III   *The Mansion*)
(1891—June, 1910)

Dashes indicate a marriage; wavy lines indicate an extra-marital union.

McCASLIN

Lucius Quintus Carothers McCaslin----Wife
(1772—June 27, 1837)

Amodeus (Buddy) | Theophilus (Buck)-~Sophonsiba Beauchamp
(–*ca.* 1869) | (–*ca.* 1869)
                         ⌐Isaac McCaslin
Daughter----Husband   (1867–?)

Daughter---Edmonds

McCaslin Edmonds---Alice
(1850–?)
          Zachary Edmonds

father of Roth

Carothers Edmonds-~Negress Beauchamp
(March 1898—   ) (granddaughter of
              Son   Tennie's Jim)

Lucius Quintus Carothers McCaslin-~~~~Eunice----Thucydus
(1772–1837)   (–1832) (1779–1854)
        Tomasina (Tomy, Tomey)(1810—June, 1833)

Lucius Quintus Carothers McCaslin-~Tomasina
(1772–1837)   (1810–33)
        Terrel (Tomy's Turl)----Tennie Beauchamp
        (June, 1833—ca. 1878)   (1838–?)

James T. Beauchamp   Sophonsiba B. Lucas Beauchamp---Molly
(December 29, 1864—?)(1869–?) (March 17,
                  1874–?)
          Child
Carothers
Edmonds-~Daughter   Daughter Henry   Nathalie—Wilkins
                              (1898–   ) (1923–   )
     Son
                     Samuel Worsham Beauchamp

Amodeus McCaslin Beauchamp   Callina   Child
(1859)   (1862–62)   (1863–?)

SARTORIS

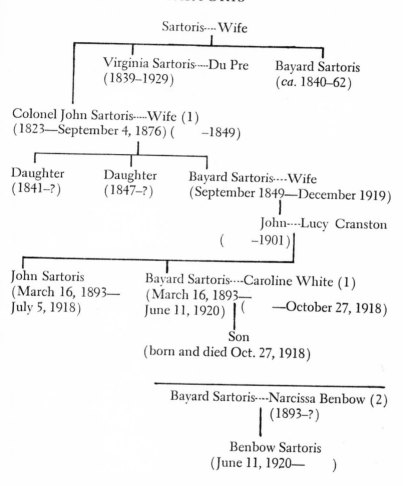

Sartoris---- Wife

Virginia Sartoris----Du Pre
(1839–1929)

Bayard Sartoris
(*ca.* 1840–62)

Colonel John Sartoris----Wife (1)
(1823—September 4, 1876) (–1849)

Daughter
(1841–?)

Daughter
(1847–?)

Bayard Sartoris----Wife
(September 1849—December 1919)

John----Lucy Cranston
(–1901)

John Sartoris
(March 16, 1893—
July 5, 1918)

Bayard Sartoris----Caroline White (1)
(March 16, 1893—
June 11, 1920) (—October 27, 1918)

Son
(born and died Oct. 27, 1918)

Bayard Sartoris----Narcissa Benbow (2)
(1893–?)

Benbow Sartoris
(June 11, 1920—   )

Colonel John Sartoris----Drusilla Hawk (2)
(1823–76)
(1841–?)

SNOPES

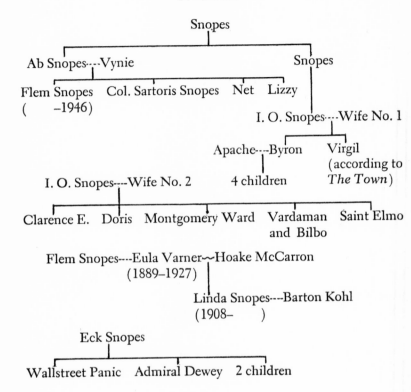

Snopes

Ab Snopes----Vynie   Snopes

Flem Snopes   Col. Sartoris Snopes   Net   Lizzy
(–1946)

I. O. Snopes----Wife No. 1

Apache----Byron   Virgil
     4 children   (according to *The Town*)

I. O. Snopes----Wife No. 2   4 children

Clarence E.   Doris   Montgomery Ward   Vardaman   Saint Elmo
                    and Bilbo

Flem Snopes----Eula Varner~Hoake McCarron
       (1889–1927)

Linda Snopes----Barton Kohl
(1908–   )

Eck Snopes

Wallstreet Panic   Admiral Dewey   2 children

Additional Snopeses: Isaac (Ike)
                       Launcelot (Lump)
                       Mink (1883–   )
                       Orestes
                       Watkins Products
                       Wesley

SUTPEN

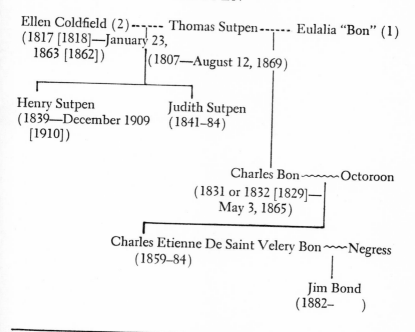

Ellen Coldfield (2) ------ Thomas Sutpen ------ Eulalia "Bon" (1)
(1817 [1818]—January 23,
1863 [1862])   (1807—August 12, 1869)

Henry Sutpen   Judith Sutpen
(1839—December 1909   (1841–84)
  [1910])

                              Charles Bon ～～～Octoroon
                        (1831 or 1832 [1829]—
                             May 3, 1865)

Charles Etienne De Saint Velery Bon ～～Negress
              (1859–84)

                              Jim Bond
                            (1882–   )

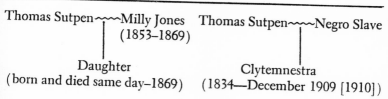

Thomas Sutpen ～～Milly Jones   Thomas Sutpen ～～Negro Slave
               (1853–1869)

         Daughter   Clytemnestra
(born and died same day–1869)   (1834—December 1909 [1910])

Brackets used for dates given by Faulkner in "Genealogy" section
of Modern Library Edition of *Absalom, Absalom!* Other dates
stem from text of novel itself.

BIBLIOGRAPHY

NOVELS

Soldiers' Pay (1926)
Mosquitoes (1927)
Sartoris (1929)
The Sound and the Fury (1929)
As I Lay Dying (1930)
Sanctuary (1931)
Light in August (1932)
Pylon (1935)
Absalom, Absalom! (1936)

The Unvanquished (1938)
The Wild Palms (1939)
The Hamlet (1940)
Intruder in the Dust (1948)
Requiem for a Nun (1951)
A Fable (1954)
The Town (1957)
The Mansion (1959)
The Reivers (1962)

COLLECTIONS

These 13 (1931). Stories included are: "Victory," "Ad Astra," "All the Dead Pilots," "Crevasse," "Red Leaves," "A Rose for Emily,"

"A Justice," "Hair," "That Evening Sun," "Dry September," "Mistral," "Divorce in Naples," "Carcassonne."

Doctor Martino and Other Stories (1934). Stories included are: "Doctor Martino," "Fox Hunt," "The Hound," "Death Drag," "There Was a Queen," "Smoke," "Turnabout," "Beyond," "Wash," "Elly," "Black Music," "Leg," "Mountain Victory," "Honor."

Go Down, Moses and Other Stories (1942). Stories included are: "Was," "The Fire and the Hearth," "Pantaloon in Black," "The Old People," "The Bear," "Delta Autumn," "Go Down, Moses."

Knight's Gambit (1949). Stories included are: "Smoke," "Monk," "Hand Upon the Waters," "Tomorrow," "An Error in Chemistry," "Knight's Gambit."

Collected Stories of William Faulkner (1950). Stories included are: "Barn Burning," "Shingles for the Lord," "Tall Men," "A Bear Hunt," "Two Soldiers," "Shall Not Perish," "A Rose for Emily," "Hair," "Centaur in Brass," "Dry September," "Death Drag," "Elly," "Uncle Willy," "Mule in the Yard," "That Will Be Fine," "That Evening Sun," "Red Leaves," "A Justice," "A Courtship," "Lo!," "Ad Astra," "Victory," "Crevasse," "Turnabout," All the Dead Pilots," "Wash," "Honor," "Doctor Martino," "Fox Hunt," "Pennsylvania Station," "Artist at Home," "The Brooch," "My Grandmother Millard," "Golden Land," "There Was A Queen," "Mountain Victory," "Beyond," "Black Music," "Leg," "Mistral," "Divorce in Naples," "Carcassonne."

Big Woods (1955). Stories included are: "The Bear," "The Old People," "A Bear Hunt," "Race at Morning."

New Orleans Sketches (1958). Sketches included are: "Mirrors of Chartres Street," "Damon and Pythias Unlimited," "Home," "Jealousy," "Cheest," "Out of Nazareth," "The Kingdom of God," "The Rosary," "The Cobbler," "Chance," "Sunset," "The Kid Learns," "The Liar," "Episode," "Country Mice," "Yo Ho and Two Bottles of Rum."